Book 1
Discovering the Bible

Revised 2018

This book belongs to:

_____

(23.8.22)

"What you have heard from me in the presence of many witnesses entrust to faithful men who will be able to teach others also."

2 Timothy 2:2

TTI Contact Information:

admin@ttionline.org

TTI Website:

www.ttionline.org

Book 1
Discovering the Bible
Revised 2018
This edition published by The Timothy Initiative

TTI Bullseye
2020–2025

LEADERS DEVELOPING LEADERS

CHURCHES PLANTING CHURCHES

DISCIPLES MAKING DISCIPLES

Every People
Every Place

UNREACHED & LEAST REACHED PEOPLES

VULNERABLE, ORPHAN, WIDOW, TRAFFICKING

SUSTAINABLE PIPELINE PRODUCING LEADERS AT EVERY LEVEL

Acknowledgements

Discovery Bible Study is a process created by David Watson a long time missionary and church planter. We thank him and the other ministries for formulating such a great process of reading and understanding the bible.

Larry Caldwell is an experienced pastor, missionary, and professor of hermeneutics. He created for TTI the seven steps guide for seeing the Bible come alive. We are eternally grateful for his gift of love and his understanding of scripture.

TTI's Board of Directors has given us freedom and focus to excel still more. We are deeply moved by these men and women of God. Our TTI investor base of financial and prayer partners extend around the globe. These individuals, churches, ministries, networks, corporations, and organizations are essential and strategic to our collective health and Kingdom impact. Thank you!

We thank the TTI Leaders around the world for your ministry of love and commitment. You are the ones that lead into new frontiers with the Gospel. You truly are our heroes.

Finally, we are forever grateful to you, the church planter. You are planting an orchard, a church-planting center through your local church that will touch your region and the world with the Gospel of Jesus Christ. We are honored to serve the Lord Jesus Christ and you. You will make a difference for our great God as you multiply healthy churches for His glory. We love you!

TTI Curriculum

This is the first workbook in TTI's core curriculum that assist in equipping church planting leaders to start churches that saturate a region and help reach every man, woman, and child with the Good News of our Lord. Below is the list of all our books.

Workbook Number/Course:

1.   Discovering the Bible

2.   Communicating the Bible

3.   The Book of Acts & Church Planting Movements

4.   Old Testament 1

5.   Old Testament 2

6.   New Testament Gospels

7.   The Heart of the Disciple Making Church Planter (Pastoral Epistles)

8.   New Testament General Letters

9.   Major Bible Doctrines

10.   Apologetics-Church History-Spiritual Warfare

Structure of this Book

This book is broken down into multiple sections.

Section 1 covers what is known as "Discovery Bible Study Methods." Discovery Bible Study is simply a method to study the Word of God. This method has been used all over the world to effectively assist disciple makers and church planters study the Bible well.

Section 2 is an introduction to interpreting and understanding the Bible. This section gives answers to important questions like: "What is the Bible?" "How did we get the Bible?" "Who wrote the Bible?" and "How do we know the Bible is complete?"

Section 3 offers a simple but practical 7-step guide to Doing Bible Interpretation. This section deals with foundational questions as to why we study the Bible and then offers a practical guide to doing so. Those who interpret the Bible need to understand the Bible is living and active. This is why the 7-steps are about, "Seeing the Bible Come Alive!" This is what good Bible interpretation is all about. It is seeing the Bible come alive.

Appendix 1 goes into greater detail into the numerous literary forms found in the Bible. Knowing the literary form of a passage has implications for the way it should be interpreted, since not all literary forms are interpreted in the same way. This section goes deeper into Bible interpretation and will be helpful for those who desire more understanding.

Appendix 2 offers additional Discovery Bible Study lessons.

Appendix 3 offers a simple to use Bible reading plan.

Table of Contents

Section 1: Discovery Bible Study Methods

Read, obey, and share – that is the discovery process.

We read God's Word out loud (if we are in a group) or write it word for word (if we are studying on our own).

Next, we put God's Words into our own words—just to make sure we really understand what His Word says and to make sure we can share it with others in different situations.

Finally, we commit to two things: to change our life so that we obey God's Word and share what God taught us with at least one other person. Obedience and sharing should happen soon. If too much time passes between reading God's Word and obeying it, people tend to disobey God and begin a habit of forgetful or careless disobedience in their lives. TTI recommends you commit to sharing what you learn with others within a day or two.

According to Scripture, if we read God's Word and disobey it we either don't love God (*John 14:15-21*) or we are foolish (*James 1:22-25, Proverbs 10:8, 14:9, 14:16*). If we don't share God's Word, can we say we love others (*John 14, Matthew 22, 1 John 3:13*)? If we know what to do, but choose not to do it, we are disobedient (*James 4:17*).

The problem is we often follow a religious system that does not anticipate or expect obedience to God's Word. We often times judge spiritual maturity by what someone knows rather than if they obey what they know. If we want to grow spiritually, adopting a system that encourages behaviors that lead to spiritual growth is the best path forward. Discovery Bible Study is one process that encourages those behaviors.

Let's take a look at how Discovery Bible Study works for personal study and group study as well as in oral and literate cultures.

Personal Discovery Bible Study

Turn a piece of paper on its side, then divide the paper into three columns. Label the first "Scripture." Label the second "My Own Words." Label the third "I Will."

SCRIPTURE   MY OWN WORDS   I WILL

Scripture

The length of the passage affects how much time the study takes. Longer passages take longer to study. This isn't a bad thing, but you need to keep it in mind. Generally, try to keep your passages between 10 and 15 verses. In the 'Scripture' column, copy the passage word-for-word (exactly how it is written in the Bible). This takes time but you control how much time by choosing smaller portions of Scripture. Break larger passages into several sections, spread out over several days. What is most important, however, is this – when you copy a passage word-for-word you actually read it through several (about five to seven) times. It is a form of forced meditation for those of us who can't sit and think about a passage without losing focus. This process also keeps us from skimming familiar passages. When you write it out you have to think about every word.

My Own Words

When you finish writing or listening to the passage, use the second column to write the passage in your own words. Write it out like you're telling a friend about it. Don't move on until you can write the passage in your own words. You see, you don't really understand it if you can't tell it to someone else in your own words. And you can't obey Scripture unless you understand it. It's that simple. Sometimes, you might have to stop on a passage for a couple of days and talk it out with the Holy Spirit before you can finish putting it into your own words. When you start this process, you will probably find there are several familiar passages that you can't write in your own words. Sometimes we 'know' more than we truly understand.

I Will

In the third column we transition from knowing God's Word to obeying God's Word. Look at each part of the passage. Ask God to reveal things you need to add to your life, take away from your life, or change in your life to obey this passage. Be specific. The passage may say that God created the Earth, but how does that impact your life? How does your life change because you believe God created the Earth? What do you need to do differently? What can you do in the next day or two to obey this passage? Every time we open God's Word, He invites us into a relationship. We call His invitation 'grace,' because we can't do anything to deserve it. Faith is how we accept His invitation. God is pleased with those who obey His Word (John 14:23-24). When we study God's Word we have a choice: we choose to obey Him or we choose to disobey Him. It is really that simple. This third column is your response to God's invitation.

Share

When you finish this study, you have two responsibilities. First, you need to meet with other followers of Christ and discuss what you learned. Tell them your 'I Will' statements. They can hold you accountable and figure out ways to help you obey God's Word. Second, look for opportunities to share what God said. You can use the phrase, "God taught me something today" or something similar, into conversations and wait for a response. This creates discussion opportunities. If people care, they ask for more information. If it isn't the right time for them, they will ignore you. Please share your faith with those who are ready and interested!

Summary:

1. Write the passage word-for-word in column 1.
2. Write the passage in your own words in column 2.
3. List the actions you must take to obey this passage in column 3.
4. Share what you learned with other believers for accountability.
5. Create discussion opportunities with not-yet-believers.
6. Share with people who are interested.

Group Discovery Bible Study

Prayer
When you meet with groups for Discovery Bible Study, go around the room and have everyone share one thing they are **thankful** for and one thing that is causing **anxiety or fear** (stressing them out). Point out to the group that one aspect of prayer is just telling God the things we are thankful for and talking with Him about what worries them or stresses them out. Transition this interaction from a group share time to an open, interactive prayer time. This form of prayer is very interactive and get the quietest people involved in group prayer.

The Holy Spirit
Right after you pray, ask the group to share what God said to them in their personal time (devotions) with Him since your last meeting. Asking this question at the beginning of every meeting encourages group members to have a personal time with God. It also reinforces and affirms every member's ability to hear God's voice. Giving them an opportunity to share allows room for the Holy Spirit to take the group study in a completely different direction than you planned. Be sensitive to the group and make sure they have this time.

Scripture
After everyone has a chance to share, have someone read Scripture out loud while everyone follows along in their Bible (or listens carefully for those without Bibles or illiterate). When they are done, have someone else read the same passage out loud again. This time have everyone listen to the reading. When they are done, ask for a volunteer to retell the passage in their own words. When they finish, ask the group to fill in any points

they feel were left out. Reading, listening, and retelling Scripture is more important than you might think.

This pattern allows different learning styles to engage (interact with) Scripture. Everyone has time to think about the passage and ask the Holy Spirit to speak through God's Word. Retelling the passage allows them to think through how they can share this passage with someone from outside the group. Allowing the group to add to the retelling encourages everyone to think about the main points in the passage. Even though going through the passage multiple times seems repetitive and time consuming, the process helps develop reproducing disciples.

Discovery Study

After your group retells the Scripture, you can study the passage. Your discussion should be filled with questions. Questions facilitate the discovery process. Questions allow your group to wrestle with (consider deeply) Scripture and grow spiritually. Below are some sample questions to encourage interaction with Scripture:

- Did anything in this passage capture your attention?
- What did you like about this passage?
- Did anything bother you? Why?
- What does this passage tell us about God?
- What does this passage tell us about Man?
- What does this passage tell us about living to please God?

Keep discussion focused on Scripture. If you or someone else in your group is knowledgeable of the Bible, it will be hard to avoid introducing outside materials into the study. You, as the facilitator, need to work hard to limit the discussion of extra-Biblical or other Biblical materials. These materials are not bad, but they don't facilitate interaction with Scripture. In most cases extra-Biblical materials emphasize the intelligence of the one introducing the materials rather than keeping Scripture at center stage. Sometimes this is not the case, but those moments are rare. Do your best to keep discussion focused on the Scripture that is the focus of the study.

Commitment

Knowledge of God's Word must translate into obedience or it is wasted. This next step begins with a statement and a question:

<u>"Since we believe God's Word is true, what must we change in our lives to obey God?"</u>

Everyone in the group must answer this question before they leave. If they already obey this Scripture, have them share how they obey it. Ask them if there is anything else they need to do to increase their obedience to God's Word in this area of their life. Keep this part of your time <u>focused on specifics</u>. For example, realizing that there is only one God is awesome, but how does that lead to action? In this case you might encourage them with a follow up question: "Now that you believe there is one God, what do you need to change in your life? What will you do differently?" Encourage your group to identify specific things to do to obey the passage.

After everyone shares how they are going to obey Scripture, have them identify someone who needs to hear what God said to the group. Encourage them to share what they learned with that person. Before you finish, ask the group to identify people they know who are in need. Ask the group to identify ways to meet those needs in the next week. Finally, close in prayer.

Summary of Group Discovery Bible Study

- Begin by having the group share one thing they are thankful for and one challenge that is stressing them out (worrying) in a group prayer process.
- Ask the group to share what God told them through His Word since the last meeting.
- Ask them to share how they were obedient to the previous week's Scripture.
- Read the week's portion of Scripture out loud while people follow along in their Bibles.
- Have someone else read the same passage out loud while the group listens.
- Have someone else in the group retell the passage in their own words. Allow the group to add to the retelling, if necessary.
- Use discovery questions to encourage the group to interact with the passage.
- Challenge the group to obey God's Word.
  - Have each person share what they are going to do to obey the passage over the next week.
- Have the group identify people they will share the passage with during the next week and write down their names.
- Have the group identify people in need and commit to meeting those needs.
- Close in prayer.

Discovery Bible Study in Oral Cultures

In oral cultures the discovery process is similar to the group process outlined above. Since they can't read, you could possibly use an audio Bible (like those provided by Faith Comes by Hearing: www.fcbh.org) or you could have someone who can read actually read the passage through for the group. Allowing the group to retell the passage is even more important in oral settings because repetition helps them remember the passage.

Why do all of these lessons say the same thing?

Great question! We are so glad you asked! The way we teach a lesson is almost as important as the lesson itself. We can choose to use teaching techniques that build a student's dependence on a teacher. Or, we can use techniques that prepare a student to stand on their own from the beginning.

The repetition you observed in these lessons is intentional. We want someone to-after only a few lessons-see this process is easy. We want them to know they can repeat the process when they study God's Word individually and when they eventually facilitate a group. A little repetition leads to rapid multiplication.

What about people who don't know Christ?

Ask everyone in the room to share something they are thankful for. Ask everyone in the room to share something that is bothering them or causing them stress. Read the Scripture passage for the day. If you have access to an audio Bible, you may choose to listen to the passage. Ask someone in the room to repeat the story. When they are done, ask the group if the person left anything important out of the story.

Ask: "What does this story tell us about God?" "What does this story tell us about man?" "What does this story tell us about what God wants to do?"

Give them time to answer. Resist the urge to tell them what the story means. If they aren't getting it, read additional passages of Scripture or ask more questions.

Ask: "If this story is true, how does that change how we act?"
Ask: "What questions do you have about this story?"
Ask: "Do you know anyone who needs to hear this story?"
Ask: "Does anyone want to accept Christ?"

Encourage them to share the story with anyone they name.

Ask: "Is there anyone you know who needs help? What can we do to help them?"

Have the group decide what needs to be done and commit to doing it before the next meeting.

Discovery Bible Study Sample Lesson

Genesis 1:1-25

Discover

- What are you thankful for this week?
- What problems do you have this week?
- Is there any way this group can help you?

Do NOT teach the below truths but ask questions until they discover the basic idea: There is a God who created the world.

- What happens in this passage?
- What does this passage tell us about God?
- What does this passage tell us about people?
- After the group has discovered truths from God's Word, help them identify what difference this makes in their lives.

Obey

Ask questions to help individuals and groups tell how their lives can change if they live like the passage is truth. Help them make specific statements about the results of any change. Help them move from a general statement to a specific statement.

- If this passage is true how does this passage change how we see God?
- If this passage is true how does this passage change how we treat others?
- If this passage is true how does this passage change how we live?
- What other questions do you have about this passage?

Share

- Do you know anyone you can share this story with?
- Do you know anyone who needs help? What can this group do to help them? Close in prayer.

From Creation to Christ
Recommended Discovery Bible Study Lessons

1. God Creates *Genesis 1:1-25*
2. God Creates Man and Woman *Genesis 2:4-24*
3. Man and Woman Eat the Fruit *Genesis 3:1-13*
4. God's Curses *Genesis 3:14-24*
5. God Regrets His Creation *Genesis 6:5-8*
6. God Saves Noah and His Family *Genesis 6:9-8:14*
7. God's Covenant with Noah *Genesis 8:15-9:17*
8. God's Covenant with Abram *Genesis 12:1-8, 15:1-6, 17:1-7*
9. Abraham Gives His Son as an Offering *Genesis 22:1-19*
10. God Spares His People *Exodus 12:1-28*
11. The Commands of God *Exodus 20:1-21*
12. The Sin Offering *Leviticus 4:1-35*
13. God's Righteous Servant *Isaiah 53*
14. Jesus is Born *Luke 1:26-38, 2:1-20*
15. Jesus is Baptized *Matthew 3; John 1:29-34*
16. Jesus is Tested *Matthew 4:1-11*
17. Jesus and the Religious Leader *John 3:1-21*
18. Jesus and the Samaritan Woman *John 4:1-26, 39-42*
19. Jesus and the Paralyzed Man *Luke 5:17-26*
20. Jesus Calms the Storm *Mark 4:35-41*
21. Jesus and the Man with Evil Spirits *Mark 5:1-20*
22. Jesus Raises a Man from the Dead *John 11:1-44*
23. Jesus Talks about His Betrayal and the Covenant *Matthew 26:17-30*
24. Jesus is Betrayed and Faces Trial *John 18:1-19:16*
25. Jesus is Crucified *Luke 23:32-56*
26. Jesus is Resurrected *Luke 24:1-35*
27. Jesus Appears to the Disciples and Ascends to Heaven *Luke 24:36-53*
28. Enter into the Kingdom God *John 3:1-21*

*More Discovery Bible Study lessons are listed in the back of the book in Appendix 2.

Section 2: Interpreting and Understanding the Bible

This Section focuses on **interpreting** and **understanding the Bible.**

Imagine finding a letter that was written 100 years ago. You do not know who wrote it or why. You do not know the person to whom the letter is written. You do not know the people, places, or even some of the words that it mentions. Now imagine you were asked to explain the letter to another person. You might be able to figure out some things, but you might make some wrong guesses as well. In order to explain the letter correctly, you would need to know more about the authors, recipients, and the purpose of the letter. It would also be helpful to know the background of the author and the recipients.

The Bible is the same. If we do not understand where the Bible came from, how it was written and why, we may make mistakes when trying to interpret and understand the Bible.

The first question we must ask is *"What is the Bible?"* The Bible is God's word written down. It carries the very breath and character of God. It is through these Holy Scriptures that God communicates with us.

Second, we ask, *"How did we get the Bible?"* God revealed Himself to people and told them to write down His words completely and accurately, free from error.

Third, we ask *"Who wrote the Bible?"* God chose 40+ people to communicate His message both orally and in writing. These stories and writings were historically written down, reproduced and shared with others. God combined His message with the words and language of the author to express the things of God. As a result, the Bible is the combination of God's thoughts communicated through human words and understanding. These writings form what we now call the Bible. The Bible is an unchanging set of stories, teachings and principles. There is nothing more to add to it. God's revealed Scripture is complete.

How do we know that the Bible is complete?

Jude 3 — This part of the Bible instructs us to *defend the faith that God has entrusted once for all time to His holy people.* This verse disagrees with anyone who tries to claim that God has given them a new revelation. ***Though the Holy Spirit certainly gives us direction in our lives, the Holy Spirit never adds to or contradicts the Bible.***

Instead of preserving the original writings of Scripture, God gave man the responsibility of protecting it, copying it, and translating it.

1. Before there were hand-written copies and printing presses, much of Scripture was communicated orally.
2. After some time, these words were written down and reproduced by individuals who copied the writings by hand. They did this as accurately as possible, and the Bible we have today is a result of those copies (see *John 14:26).*

This shows why the Bible is worthy to be trusted as a guide of our faith. The Bible gives all people the opportunity to hear and read God's Word regardless of their language. **The Bible is the most translated book ever!**

Who was the Bible written to?

The Bible was written to all mankind. Through God's Spirit and His Word, He reveals Himself to us. <u>The Bible is God's Word!</u> The purpose and goal of God's communication with us is so we can be in a relationship with and worship Him. When we read, hear, and obey the Word of God this must be our ultimate goal.

Interpreting and understanding the Bible is extremely important because most everything we know about God and Christ comes from His Word. If you do not understand it, or if you interpret it incorrectly, you can mislead yourself as well as those you teach. Also, consider how your culture is different from the cultures in which the Bible was written, so it is your job to interpret Scripture in your context.

One of the primary roles of a disciple who makes disciples is to give proper attention to both the meaning of Scripture and its application in their culture. We pray your disciples will bear spiritual fruit and grow. This section will help you on your mission!

The Beginning

The first person introduced in the Bible is God. The first human being mentioned is a man named Adam. He was the first human of God's creation. Created perfect, he lived in a faultless garden named Eden. God said it was not good for this man to be alone, so He created a perfect woman named Eve. Adam and Eve enjoyed the garden, a perfect relationship with each other, and direct communication with God. There was one tree in the garden God told them not to eat from, but Satan, disguised as a serpent, came and deceived them. They ate from the tree, disobeying God's command. Disobedience is sin. This sin broke the relationship they had with God and with each other. They felt fear and shame, so they hid themselves. God, who was their Father and Friend, became their Judge. There was now separation and they no longer had direct access in their relationship with God *(Genesis 1-3).*

All humans originate from this first man and woman (Adam and Eve). As a result of their sin, all people have a broken relationship with God. In this state we cannot have a proper relationship with God.

For Example: On a cloudy day, you cannot see the sun or the moon or the stars above you. They are blocked from your vision. However, when the clouds go away you can see everything that you could not see before. Through the Bible, God reveals Himself to us so that we may see Him. He has chosen to reveal many things to us in the Bible, including His Son, Jesus. Apart from Jesus revealing Himself, we cannot see God or know Him. **Fortunately, God provided a way to remake the broken relationship with us!** The way we learn about fixing this relationship is through God's Word. (We call this process Revelation.)

1. The Problem: We are separated from God and cannot see Him *(Isaiah 55:8; 1 Corinthians 2:9).*
2. The Goal: To be in proper relationship with God. The way we do this is by knowing Jesus Christ and becoming more like Him *(Romans 8:28; 2 Corinthians 3:18).*
3. The Reason: When we become like Jesus Christ, our sins are covered and our lives experience transformation *(1 John 2:6).*
4. The Result: The glory of God is evident in and through our lives *(2 Corinthians 3:18; Psalm 96:3).*

Example: Imagine you are walking along the road and you see a man jumping up and down waving his hands in the air. One person might see this man and think, "That man needs help."

Another person might pass by and think, "That man is drunk." A third person might look at him and say, "That man has been kicked out of the village." There can be as many interpretations of that man's actions as there are people walking down the road. However, we can't know what his behavior really means unless he explains it to us.

The Bible tells us everything we need to know about how God can fix our relationship with Him, through His Son, Jesus.

1. Jesus came to Earth as a person to reveal God to the World.
2. The Old Testament was the preparation for Jesus, and everything in the New Testament was an explanation of Jesus.

Assignment: Practice telling the story of Adam and Eve. After telling the story answer the following questions:

1. What do we learn about God?
2. What do we learn about Man?
3. What principles do we learn, or what sins should we avoid?
4. What commands are there to obey, or examples to follow?
5. What is my response? What must I do?
6. Who should I share this with?

Application Points for the week:

By answering these questions, you are interpreting and applying the Bible! A simple and easy tool to use when interpreting the Bible is called the SWORD method. Both the Discovery Bible Study and SWORD method are effective ways to study God's Word.

*"The Word of God is living and active, sharper than any **double-edged sword**. It penetrates even to dividing of soul and spirit, joints and marrow; it judges the thoughts and attitudes of the heart" (Hebrews 4:12).*

Everything we need to know about God and man is revealed in the Bible. The Bible also reveals God's desire for us through examples and commands we should follow. Anyone who wants to know God and follow Jesus must read the Bible and seek to follow its commands.

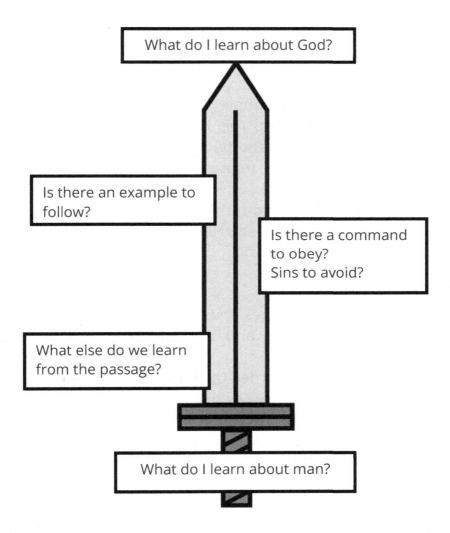

When the Bible is read, we can learn it's meaning by asking these questions based on the above picture:

The top of the sword points toward God. We ask the question: **What do I learn about God?**

The bottom part of the sword points us toward man. We ask the question: **What do I learn about man?**

19

The two edges of the sword penetrate our lives, creating change. They lead us to ask the questions: **What principles do we learn, or what sins should we avoid? What commands are there to obey, or examples to follow?**

The side arrows on the handle of the sword direct us to the sections before and after. This is the context and gives the complete understanding and background of a verse or group of verses. You are not free to use verses however you want.

What else do we learn from this passage?
We now know that God reveals Himself to us through His Word (the Bible) and the Holy Spirit.

1. <u>God's Word:</u>
    - The words, messages and stories in the Bible are God breathed (inspired and without error) and perfectly accurate.
    - Although men recorded the Bible, its words are the very words of God.
    - The Apostle Paul and all the writers speak, but not with their own wisdom. Instead they reflect the wisdom of God *(1 Corinthians 2:6-15)*.

2. <u>Holy Spirit:</u>
    - *1 Corinthians 2:6-15* reminds us that to know the mind of God, He must tell us. No one knows the thoughts of God except the Spirit of God.
    - *John 16:7-13*: We generally believe that life would be easier and decisions simpler if Jesus was standing beside us. But even when Jesus was on the Earth He said it is good for us to have the Holy Spirit as our Comforter and Guide.

<u>Summary</u>

The main point is that we must know we are helpless apart from God. We cannot know about God without His gracious involvement on our behalf. If we forget this point we can wander towards a religion that emphasizes our own work, ability and intelligence. We must be careful not to do this!

Some Basics of Interpreting the Bible

As a result of God's communication process, we have a miracle book, unlike any book in the world. It is the only one of its kind. It is just as true as God standing in front of you and speaking directly to you. God has protected His Word so that it will guide us in the right direction. Always remember that Scripture interprets Scripture. If you are unclear on one verse or one chapter, look for other verses and chapters on the same subject to compare and contrast. For example, Luke 8:5 is interpreted by Luke 8:11-12.

1. Using the SWORD method of interpreting and understanding the Bible will guide towards proper interpretation.
2. As a result of carefully applying what we learn in the Bible, we develop correct doctrine and correct experience.
   - **Doctrine** that we receive from Scripture is built on the foundation of proper interpretation.
   - **Experience** grows out of good doctrine. This experience or application will be consistent with Scripture and foundational beliefs.
   - To consider this relationship another way, imagine the process as a house. Interpretation would be the foundation, doctrine would be the building that rests upon interpretation, and experience would be the roof that rests upon doctrine. Consider the house in the space below (or draw one for yourself) and use it to explain this principle to others.

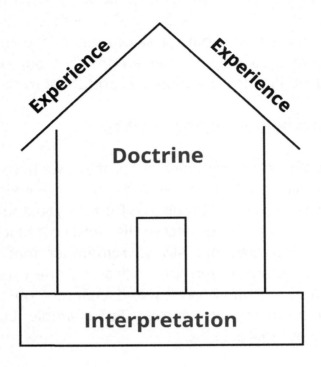

Remember, there is only *one* interpretation of a passage, but there are many applications. We must simply make sure our applications grow directly out of correct doctrine, and correct interpretation.

Caution: Be careful not to begin with Experience. A roof makes a poor foundation. Do not reverse the order. Do not work from experience to establish principles, and then develop an interpretation. When you begin with experience, you will not be able to interpret Scripture clearly. The house drawn above is the structure we are seeking to build. Make sure you understand this before moving on!

Why is it important to learn how to Interpret the Bible?
Consider the following story:

One day there was an Ethiopian returning home from a religious pilgrimage. He read from the book of Isaiah in the

Bible but was unable to understand what he was reading. God sent a man named Philip to interpret and explain what he was reading. Philip asked him, "Do you understand what you are reading?" The Ethiopian said, "How can I understand unless someone tells me?" Philip then gave a proper interpretation of the passage. As a result, the Ethiopian put his faith in Christ. (For the full story see Acts 8 and Isaiah 53.)

After discussing this story, answer the questions below:

1. What do we learn about God?

2. What do we learn about Man?

3. What principles do we learn, or what sins should we avoid?

4. What commands are there to obey, or examples to follow?

5. What is my response? What must I do?

6. Who should I share this with?

Application Points for the week:

From the story above we learn several things.

First of all, seeing words on a page of the Bible does not mean the reader can understand them. **Observing what the Bible says is only the first step of interpretation.**

Secondly, this story reminds us that proper guidance can help someone interpret the Bible. Like the Ethiopian, the meaning of the words is not always easily apparent without direction from another Bible student.

Consider the Biblical Background:

1. **The Bible's Unity**: There is great variety in the Bible. The Bible was written in many forms, by many authors, on a variety of subjects over two thousand years. There is a common subject, a common purpose, and no contradictions.

2. **The Bible's Worldview**: The Bible has a God-centered worldview. This means that everything in Scripture views the world through the eyes of God. **God gives meaning to all experiences**. He determines what man is, what knowledge is, what meaning is and what nature is.

Culture

When reading the Bible it is always important to consider the culture of the author, how your own culture impacts your interpretation, as well as the perspective of the culture that you will communicate the Word of God.

Application

Application is communicating the present-day importance of a Biblical text. Specifically, how that passage may be put into action, and inviting and urging the hearers to do what they understand. It is only through the leading and guiding of the Holy Spirit that we can fully understand and apply the truth of the Bible.

It does little good to know the truths of Scripture yet fail to put them into practice. *James 2:19* tells us that even the demons believe in God! What separates us from them is whether our lives are changed by what we know and obey. **It is not enough to have the right interpretation if that interpretation has no impact on your life or on those around you. Application is ultimately what matters to God. We must take the Truth of God and help others move from understanding to action.**

<u>Assignment</u>: **Read the story below.**

Once there was a man on a long journey. On the way he was attacked by thieves, beaten up, and left for dead. Many people passed by, including religious leaders and important people, yet no one cared for him. There was one man though, a foreigner that was not accepted well in that country, who found the man. This foreigner stopped his journey and took care of the bleeding man. He attended to his wounds and needs as well as paid for his expenses to make sure he was brought back to health. (See Luke 10:25-37.)

The questions below have been answered as an example of using the SWORD method. Consider the questions and answers below.

1. **What do we learn about God?**
   - God is a merciful God and expects us to show mercy to others in need.
   - God's expectations are not determined by color, caste, tribe, or religion.

- God expects us to love Him and love others as we love ourselves.
- Our love is expected to be shown in our actions not just our words.

2. **What do we learn about Man?**
   - The heart of man is wicked, selfish, and lacks compassion.
   - Man does not please God by simply being religious.
   - Man looks to earn favor and salvation by their works or merit.
   - Man has his own standards established by him and others.

3. What principles do we learn, or what sins should we avoid?
   - Not helping someone in need is actually hurting someone in need.
   - Sins to avoid: stealing, attacking, and taking advantage of others.
   - We should love God and others just as we love ourselves, including those of other tribes, castes and races.
   - Care for those in need.

4. What commands are there to obey, or examples to follow?
   - Follow the example of the foreigner, considering the needs of others more than your own needs.
   - Jesus said: "Go and do likewise."

5. What is my response? What must I do? Application Points for the week:
   - I will love the Lord and others as I love myself and encourage others to do the same. I will show this love by:

- Evaluating the needs of the community, actively sharing the Gospel and showing the love of Christ in word and actions.
  o Offer food to my neighbor in need.
  o Offer shelter to the orphan without a home.
  o Take the sick person in my village to the hospital.
  o Help the old man of the community in his duties.

6. Who should I share this with?

Practical Assignment: Above we asked what the passage says, what it means, and what we should do in response. To take it one step farther consider to yourself before you go to bed each day: What did I Do? How did I apply it in my life? Was I faithful and obedient to God's word? If not, what can I do tomorrow?

What is the Bible? <u>Answer</u>: It is God's Word, written down. It is the way that He communicates with us.

How did we get the Bible? <u>Answer</u>: Inspiration: The words in the Bible are God breathed…they are completely accurate and free from error.

God's breath → writers = Bible

How was the Bible transmitted? <u>Answer</u>: The Bible was communicated orally…and historically written down and reproduced.

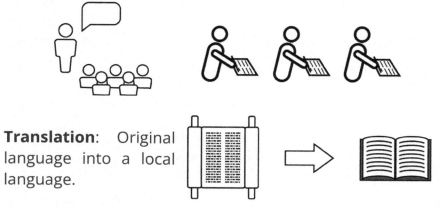

Translation: Original language into a local language.

Section 3: Basic Foundations & Seven Steps for Doing Effective and Accurate Biblical Interpretation

Why We Study the Bible

We are thankful that you desire to grow in your understanding of God's Word! Your desire is a good one. Understanding and applying God's Word, the Bible, is foundational for anyone desiring to be a disciple maker and church planter. The apostle Paul, one of the primary writers of the New Testament, wrote correctly and accurately that interpreting God's Word is very important. Paul wrote the following words to his young pastor friend, Timothy:

> *"Do your best to present yourself to God as one approved, a worker who has no need to be ashamed, rightly handling the word of truth" (2 Timothy 2:15).*

These words to Timothy apply to disciple makers and church planters today. This book on Doing Bible Interpretation will give you the tools to "rightly handle" or correctly understand and share God's Word.

What is the best way to interpret and understand the Bible? In order to understand God's Word we need to interpret and understand correctly. To interpret something is simply to explain it, or to tell its meaning, and then to communicate it in ways that are understandable to others. To communicate the Bible correctly we must be able to explain it in ways that are comprehensible. This is a main focus in Bible interpretation for disciple makers and church planters.

The apostle Paul said something else about God's Word; something that is important to understand before we begin a study on Bible interpretation:

"All Scripture is breathed out by God and profitable for teaching, for reproof, for correction, and for training in righteousness, that the man of God may be competent, equipped for every good work" (2 Timothy 3:16-17).

Several things should be understood about these two verses:

1. "All Scripture" means: all of the Bible. This means both the Old Testament and New Testament. Whether genealogies, or laws, or proverbs, or stories, or worship songs—all of Scripture is important for disciples of Christ.

2. All of this Scripture is "breathed out by God," or as some translations say, "God-breathed." God, the Holy Spirit, was involved in the making of His Word, the Bible. You are very close to somebody if you can actually feel their breath when they breathe on you. Imagine when someone breathes, that is exactly what the Lord did, He breathed not only on the original texts but in them. The original Biblical manuscripts contain the very character of God, His very breath. This is how close God was to the making of the Bible. This shows us that the Bible is important to God and it needs to be important to us as well.

3. All of Scripture is "profitable" and useful. We are not to try to understand it on an academic level, only. Rather the Bible is to be understood by us in mind, soul, and spirit so that it will be useful to us. Useful for what? Useful "for teaching, for reproof, for correction, and for training in righteousness." We seek to understand the Bible so that it will be useful in our lives as we witness and share the Love of God and Gospel to others. It is also very profitable in the

disciple making process through the lives of other Christians and churches.

4. All of this Scripture is useful in our lives "that the man of God may be complete, equipped for every good work." Do you want to be a successful disciple maker or church planter? Then you want to better understand the Bible. Why? Because the Bible will help you to "be complete" and to be "equipped for every good work." What could be a better "good work" to be "equipped" for than being a disciple maker or church planter?

This is Good News! God wants you to be fully equipped to do the very best job as a disciple maker and church planter that He has called you to do. God wants you to better understand His Word so that you can better model, mentor, teach, and train others in your role as a disciple maker and church planter. This is what doing Bible interpretation is all about.

In this section we will learn some of the basic foundations and steps concerning how to do good Bible interpretation. In Part 4 we will put these principles to work as we actively do Bible interpretation together. So let's get started!

Practical Assignment: Before you begin, consider: How has the Word of God been profitable and useful to you in your relationship with God? How have you used the Word of God where it was profitable and useful for others? Discuss and write down some answers below.

Basic Foundations

1. **The Bible is Accurate and Reliable—Directly from God**

The foundation that most Christians trust in is this: The Bible is the trustworthy Word of God that guides everything we believe and everything we do. This means the Bible is completely accurate and reliable, and comes directly from God Himself. TTI accepts the authority of the Bible as fact and will not attempt to prove it here. TTI Books #9 and #10 discuss in more detail why the Bible is truth and why Christians should believe so. As we have already seen, the fact that the Bible is *"breathed by God" (2 Timothy 3:16)* gives us a good idea of its power and authority for our lives and for the lives of our people. When God's very character is in and upon the Scriptures, then the Word has complete authority over all our lives. This is partially why the Bible is called the Word of God.

It is also important to see that only the Bible has such power and authority. While we can learn many good things about God from other books and other people outside of the Bible, it is only the Bible that is authoritative. The writer of the last book of the New Testament, the book of Revelation, makes this very clear:

> *"I warn everyone who hears the words of the prophecy of this book: if anyone adds to them, God will add to him the plagues described in this book, and if anyone takes away from the words of the book of this prophecy, God will take away his share in the tree of life and in the holy city, which are described in this book" (Revelation 22:18-19).*

The truth of these words applies to the entire Bible. The writer of the book of Jude, also in the New Testament, speaks about the fact that the giving of authoritative truth ended in New Testament times. Jude speaks to his readers *"to contend for the faith that was once for all delivered to the saints" (Jude 3)*.

As a result, everything that we need to know spiritually is already found in the Bible.

<u>The Bible **alone** is our final authority.</u>

Question: Are there any other books that are equal to the Bible?

Assignment: If the Bible is the most important book and directly from God to man: **will you commit to reading the Bible each day?** In the back of this book is a Bible reading plan that you can start using today! It is important for every disciple maker to know God's Word. Discuss as a group and write down the names of two people you will keep accountable to read their Bible.

1. _____

2. _____

2. **God Communicates His Truth to us through the Bible**

As we have already seen in the Introduction, *"All Scripture...is profitable for teaching, for reproof, for correction, and for training in righteousness" (2 Timothy 3:16)*. This means: Everything we need to know about God—what is "profitable" or "useful"—has been revealed to us in the Bible. These "profitable" things are God's Truth that He wants to make known to each one of us. God's Truth is communicated to us through the Bible.

God communicates His Truth through His Word. He also wants **EVERY Christian** to understand His Word. This is why learning how to clearly interpret the Bible is so important for disciple makers and church planters.

You who are disciple makers and church planters have two key responsibilities:

1. **Help your disciples and new believers better understand the Truth of God's Word.**

2. **Help your disciples and new believers better interpret the Bible for themselves and their families and others.**

This course will help you succeed at both of these responsibilities.

3. **Jesus is the Heart of the Bible**

The introductory words in the book of Hebrews are important as we interpret the Bible:

"Long ago, at many times and in many ways, God spoke to our fathers by the prophets, but in these last days He has spoken to us by his Son, whom He appointed the heir of all things, through whom also He created the world" (Hebrews 1:1-2).

These verses show that in the Old Testament times God spoke to His people through prophets, but in New Testament times God spoke to His people in a final way through His Son, Jesus Christ. The Old Testament prepared everyone for Jesus and the New Testament gives a clearer understanding of who Jesus is, and what he has done. As a result, Jesus is really the heart of the Bible. As we interpret both the Old and New Testaments we will need to see our interpretations with Jesus in our minds. **Question**: Discuss how you can interpret the Bible with Jesus in your thoughts. Consider the following verses as you discuss: *Genesis 3:15; 9:27; 12:2-3; 49:8-12; Numbers 24:15-19;* and *Deuteronomy 18:15-18.*

4. **The Holy Spirit Guides Biblical Interpretation**

Since the Bible is God's authoritative Word, it is good to know that we are not alone when we attempt to understand the Bible. We have a helper (Holy Spirit) who has promised *"to guide you into all the truth" (John 16:13).* The Holy Spirit is able to help as He can impact the very center of our thinking and emotions, and lead us to the Truth. Through the illuminating (revealing/making clear) work of the Holy Spirit, the Bible is made more understandable for believers *(John 15:26).* The apostle Paul makes this clear in his letter to the Christians located in the city of Corinth:

"Now we have received not the spirit of the world, but the Spirit who is from God, that we might understand the things freely given us by God. And we impart this in words not taught by human wisdom but taught by the Spirit, interpreting spiritual truths to those who are spiritual" (1 Corinthians 2:12-13).

Paul's words here show us that the Holy Spirit is with us to lead us and guide us as we interpret the Bible. We do not interpret alone.

This is critically important to understand from the very beginning! Why? Because as we realize the truth that the Bible is "breathed out by God," we also realize that God, has given us His Holy Spirit to guide us in our understanding of what His Truth is and how it applies today.

Oftentimes, courses and books on Biblical interpretation teach a lot of human-made rules and instructions. They then mostly forget about the role of the Holy Spirit. In this course we will learn a few human-made rules and instructions. We must always remember that:

Our interpretation of the Bible must always be guided by the Holy Spirit!

Biblical interpretation is **both** a Spirit-led and thinking process. Both parts of the process are important as we interpret the Bible. To emphasize the one without the other is to do injustice to God. He gave us the Holy Spirit, as well as our human minds, so that we can use both to help us better interpret the Bible.

5. Bible Interpretation is Best Done in Community

Biblical interpretation is not to be done isolated or away from other believers. It is not simply a private discipline. We can learn much about the Bible in our own private devotions and study, but it is especially *in community with other believers* where good Biblical interpretation occurs. We need a local community of believers—in small group fellowships, or in small house churches—to help us.

Proverbs 27:17: "Iron sharpens iron, and one man sharpens another." This is very true when it comes to Bible interpretation. We need each other to help us gain greater insights into Bible texts as we listen to others who are also guided by the Holy Spirit.

We observe this in at least two places in the book of Acts in the New Testament. The early church, at its very beginning, was a community of believers who did things together:

> *"And they devoted themselves to the apostles teaching and fellowship" (Acts 2:42).*

Later on in the book of Acts, the writer talks about a group of Jews who lived in the city of Berea. They listened to the apostle Paul's words about Jesus and studied the Scriptures together to better understand the truth of what Paul was saying:

> *"Now these Jews...received the word with all eagerness, examining the Scriptures daily to see if these things were so" (Acts 17:11).*

The example of the Bereans above is a good one for all of us who study God's Word. Biblical interpretation is best done with a community of believers who are all listening to the Holy Spirit and examining the Bible together in order to discover God's will for their lives.

6. Biblical Interpretation is Living and Active

Biblical interpretation is lively! It is active! *Hebrews 4:12* says,

> *"For the word of God is living and active, sharper than any two-edged sword..."*

The writer of Hebrews says that the Bible is *"living and active."* It is not dead and lazy. In fact, it is so living and active that it can cut us, *"sharper than any two-edged sword."* In doing so, the Word of God reaches the thoughts and attitudes of the heart, and reveals what is spiritual and what is from the flesh. As a result, this *"living and active"* Bible has practical applications for us as we live our lives today.

We have entitled this course **"Doing Bible Interpretation"** for good reason. Bible interpretation should be dynamic! Bible interpretation should be refreshing! This kind of ***active*** Bible interpretation motivates those who are Bible interpreters to dig deeply into this Bible that's both "God-breathed" and "useful." How exciting!

In this course you will be ***actively*** learning how to better interpret God's Word. This means more than just reading, but actively interpreting the Bible and obeying what is learned as well as sharing it with others.

At the end of many sections in this course you will get the opportunity at **"Seeing the Bible Come Alive"** so that we can all immediately apply what we have just read.

Interpreting the Bible is one of the most exciting things that church planters and disciple makers get to do. What a privilege!

7. **The Primary Purpose of Bible Interpretation is to Make Disciples**

Good Biblical interpretation is done not for its own sake, but to serve.

Our hope for all disciple makers and church planters is this: that you will better learn to "rightly handle" God's Word for one primary purpose:

For you, and the people in your churches, to be better equipped to make disciples that make disciples.

This purpose directly connects us to Jesus. At the end of His ministry on earth, He commanded all His followers to:

"Go therefore and make disciples of all nations, baptizing them in the name of the Father and of the Son and of the Holy Spirit, teaching them to observe all that I have commanded you. And behold, I am with you always, to the end of the age" (Matthew 28:19-20).

We are commanded by Jesus to "make disciples" and to teach them to obey all that Jesus commanded. As a result:
- Accurate Bible interpretation is part of being missional and intentional with our lives.
- Accurate Bible interpretation helps us to make healthy disciples.

May this course help you become better equipped to make disciples among all the nations and people groups of our world!

Conclusion

At the heart of accurate biblical interpretation is the truth that God's Word is a unique and authoritative body of writings that, with the assistance of the Holy Spirit, helps guide Christians today in what they should believe and do. <u>The Bible is God's Truth to people today.</u> Though there may be aspects of truth found in other religious writings, the Bible is uniquely God's Truth since the Scriptures point to Jesus. Only Jesus is *"the Way, and the Truth, and the Life" (John 14:6).*

As we seek to actively interpret the Bible, with the guidance of the Holy Spirit and in community with other believers, we will be better able to understand God's Word for our own lives and the lives of our families, churches, and communities. As a result, we will be better able to make disciples of all the nations.

Review Questions & Further Discussion:

1. God was intimately involved in the making of the Bible ("breathed out by God"). How does this give you confidence as you attempt to communicate the truths of the Bible to others?

2. What are two practical steps you will need to make in your own study of the Bible that will allow the Holy Spirit to play a bigger role?

3. The Bible says, "Iron sharpens iron." As a disciple maker and church planter, how will the people you are planting a church among influence your study of the Bible?

4. The purpose of Bible interpretation is to make disciples. How does this make you feel in your role as a disciple maker and church planter?

Practical Assignment: one way to grow in any area is to practice. As you begin to communicate the truths of the Bible to others consider how you will communicate these things. One practical way is to place a chair in front of you. Imagine someone is sitting there and you are explaining a truth from the Bible. How can you communicate in a way that is clear and easy to understand? What can you do to make your words more simple and practical?

Seeing the Bible Come Alive
Steps 1 and 2

You who are disciple makers and church planters desire a good thing. You desire to interpret the Bible for your own life, and for the lives of those you lead in the best way you can. This book is designed to help you do just that.

Those who interpret the Bible need to understand the Bible is living and active when they attempt to understand it. That's why the next few sections are titled, "Seeing the Bible Come Alive!" This is what good Bible interpretation is all about. It is seeing the Bible come alive both for ourselves, as well as for those with whom we interpret.

Do you want your Bible interpretation to come alive? We certainly hope so! For this to happen, a good interpreter will ask the following seven questions. We call these questions: **Seven Steps to Seeing the Bible Come Alive!**

Step 1: What kind of literary style is this Bible passage and what are the implications of this?

Step 2: What is the context of the Bible passage?

Step 3: What was God saying through this Bible passage to the original audience?

Step 4: What is the general principle that God had in mind through this Bible passage for all peoples and all cultures?

Step 5: What is God saying through this Bible passage to you today?

Step 6: What is God saying through this Bible passage to your community of believers today?

Step 7: How will you communicate the truths of this Bible passage to your community of believers?

Let's get started!

Step 1 to Seeing the Bible Come Alive!

What kind of literary style is this Bible passage and what are the implications of this?

The first question to ask when trying to understand a passage of Scripture is simple: What kind of literary style or form is the passage? Knowing the literary form of a passage has implications for the way it should be interpreted, since not all literary forms are interpreted in the same way.

So what do we mean by the phrase "literary style or form"? Let's look at a practical example.

We would all agree that reading a newspaper is very different from reading a love letter from your spouse. They both are forms of communication, but you "read" or interpret a newspaper in a different way than you "read" or interpret a love letter. When reading a newspaper you look for information, pictures and so on. When reading a love letter you look for key words like "I love you," and so on. You may even read it many times and share it with others. In other words, you use different mental categories when you attempt to understand these two very different forms of communication.

All literary styles and forms are like this. They all have certain ways that they are to be read. So, for example, we interpret the various Old Testament laws differently than we do when we interpret the stories and parables of Jesus. Both law and parables are unique literary forms and have different literary "rules" that we use to interpret them. The same is true for all the different literary forms that are found in the Bible.

In Appendix 1 we examine different literary forms in more detail and how to interpret them. They include:

1. Story or narrative
2. Law
3. Poetry, especially Psalms and Proverbs
4. Prophecy
5. Sayings of Jesus
6. Parables of Jesus
7. Letters to churches or Epistles
8. Apocalyptic, especially the book of Revelation

Step 2 to Seeing the Bible Come Alive!

__What is the context of the Bible passage?__

Before we talk about the context of the Bible passage we must first answer what we mean by the word "context." Context describes the setting, background or situation of a passage.

For example, consider the following statement and discuss if your answer is yes or no: "I have an extra one, would you like me to share with you?

Without knowing what it is that the person is offering makes it difficult to decide the answer. If it is a hot day and the item is a bottle of water, the answer will likely be yes. However, if it is at the market and the item is stolen goods, the answer should be no. Do you see why the context of what is happening is so important?

This is why taking a verse out of its context is not a wise thing to do. With no context to understand the verse there is an incomplete understanding of what that verse means. No context means we will have an incomplete understanding.

No Context = Incomplete Understanding

Let's look at another example. The five words below were found in the headline of a newspaper. What does this headline mean?

"Child Killed in Motorbike Accident"

There are at least two possibilities to this headline's meaning. It could mean that a child was wandering in the streets, and was then hit by a passing motorbike. Or, this headline could mean that a child was riding on the motorbike, got into an accident, and was killed. Again, which interpretation is correct? We will never know by reading the headline alone. The only way that we will know what the headline means is if we read the rest of the story. It is in the rest of the story where we will find more of the facts and details surrounding the accident. Only with more information from the article will we be able to understand what the headline is saying. Usually the more context we have the more understanding we will also have.

More Context = More Understanding

In the case of the Bible, when we use the word "context," we refer to the words, phrases or sentences that surround a particular Bible passage that help give understanding to that passage. Properly understanding the Bible context also includes what we call "setting the contextual boundaries." In other words, when we first attempt to understand a particular Bible passage, we want to determine where that passage begins and where it ends. Sometimes our Bible interpretations will be different, depending on where the contextual boundaries are set.

Another thing to remember when setting contextual boundaries is this: all the chapter, verse, paragraph and section headings that are found in most of our Bibles today were added much later. They were added after the Bible was written. They are not a part of the original writing of the Bible. As a result, we need to set the contextual boundaries where they really exist, not where the chapter and verse numbers are.

Let's look at two examples of why the setting of contextual boundaries is so important in Bible interpretation.

Two Examples of the Importance of Setting Contextual Boundaries

A. **Example #1: _Psalm 50:10_**

"For every beast of the forest is mine, the cattle on a thousand hills."

This verse is oftentimes interpreted in the wrong context, with no regard to its contextual boundaries. Taking the verse out of context leads many Christians to interpret the verse something like the following:

What God is saying to me in this verse is this: He owns everything in the world, even the cattle on a thousand hills. As a result, what this verse is saying is that God wants to bless all Christians, especially me, with material blessings. Since God owns so many cattle, He can certainly spare just one cow for my own needs.

Seen in the absence of its overall context, Psalm 50:10 is viewed by many as a verse of blessing: God wants to bless us with material goods since He owns everything in the first place. However, when this verse is seen in the entire context of Psalm 50—its contextual boundaries—we get an entirely different understanding. In the context of the entire Psalm 50 what God is saying is more like this:

- God is calling His faithful ones to Himself (verses 1-6).
- He is testifying against them (verse 7), reminding them that He does not need their sacrifices and offerings (verses 8 and 9).
- He is not the kind of God that is hungry and needs to eat (verses 12-13). Rather "every beast of the forest" is His, as are "the cattle on a thousand hills" (verse 10); in fact

He knows "all the birds of the hills" and "all that moves in the field" are His (verse 11).

- Those faithful ones, who do "offer to God a sacrifice of thanksgiving" and who call upon Him "in the day of trouble" will be delivered (verses 14-15), they will be shown "the salvation of God" (verse 23).
- But the wicked unfaithful ones have no right to offer sacrifices. They will be rebuked and torn apart "and there will be none to deliver" them (verses 16-22).

As a result of looking at the overall context of Psalm 50 we see that **verse 10 is not a verse about material blessings**. Rather, *it's a verse found in the overall context of obedience or judgment.* God owns everything and expects obedience and does not need anything from humans. He is calling His faithful ones to offer true sacrifices of thanksgiving in obedience to His laws. When they do this they will be blessed.

Just looking at *Psalm 50:10* by itself, without paying attention to its contextual boundaries, gives us an incomplete understanding of what God is saying in this verse. By looking at the verse in the total context of Psalm 50, however, we get a much clearer understanding about what God is speaking about in the one verse of Psalm 50:10.

Take some time as a group and discuss this together.

B. **Example #2: *Revelation 3:20***

> *"Behold, I stand at the door and knock. If anyone hears My voice and opens the door, I will come in to him and eat with him, and he with me."*

Revelation 3:20 is often interpreted out of context. Why? It's because the interpreter fails to set the contextual boundaries.

How do we usually interpret this verse? Oftentimes we use this verse when presenting the Gospel in an evangelizing encounter. We say something like this to the non-Christian when using *Revelation 3:20*: "Jesus is standing at the door of your heart and is knocking. All you have to do is to open the door of your heart and you can receive him." But is this a correct understanding of what Jesus is saying in this verse in the overall contextual boundaries of Revelation chapter 3?

- In the overall context of chapters 1 to 3, John, the writer of the book of Revelation, is addressing his words "to the seven churches that are in Asia" *(Revelation 1:4).*
- For most of the churches there are words of encouragement but also words of judgment. John tells the seven churches to "hear what the Spirit says to the churches" and to "conquer" over the real obstacles that the believers of these churches faced.
- In this overall context comes the *Revelation 3:20* passage, in the immediate context of John's word to the church *(Revelation 3:14-23)*. Here the believers are described as being "neither cold nor hot" *(Revelation 3:15)* and because they "are lukewarm, and neither hot nor cold, I will spit you out of my mouth" *(Revelation 3:16).*
- But there is hope for these believers: "Those whom I love, I reprove and discipline, so be zealous and repent" *(Revelation 3:19)*. If these believers repent, they can have fellowship with God once again, even the intimacy of table fellowship (eating a meal together with others).
- Jesus is standing at the door and knocking. The believer just has to hear His voice and open the door; then Jesus will come in to the repentant believer and eat with him.

So, is *Revelation 3:20* a verse for **unbelievers** or for **believers**?

Take some time as a group and discuss this together.

Taken only by itself, out of context and without contextual boundaries, we have an incomplete understanding. However, in the fuller context of the entire passage, verse 3:20 looks much different. In its context it's definitely not a verse for unbelievers. It's a verse for believers who are currently out of fellowship with Jesus.

There is great hope for these believers: they can repent and hear Jesus like he is knocking at the door of their house. They just have to open that door and they can have fellowship with Him like they are eating together around the table in their house.

Remember: more context equals more understanding. The verse was originally used to encourage backsliding believers to repent and have their fellowship with Jesus restored once again. The opening of the door, and the resulting table fellowship, are powerful pictures of restored relationship. We miss this when we take the verse out of context and fail to set contextual boundaries.

Conclusion

Many of us who are church planters and disciple makers have favorite Bible verses. That's a good thing. However, by not setting contextual boundaries we may take many of these favorite Bible verses out of context. When we do this, we may have an incomplete understanding of what God is trying to say to us in the particular verse. We may even have a mistaken understanding of what God is trying to say in the passage.

You should now have a good idea of what is meant by the literary form of a Bible passage. You should also understand the importance of context and setting contextual boundaries when interpreting the Bible.

These are Steps 1 and 2 of the "Seven Steps to See the Bible Come Alive!"

Review Questions
1. Can you think of two reasons why the literary form of a Bible passage might impact how that passage is interpreted?
2. Why is context and setting contextual boundaries so important to remember when interpreting the Bible?
3. How have you interpreted Psalm 50:10 in the past? How will viewing the verse in its total context give you more understanding of how to interpret the verse?
4. Have you ever used Revelation 3:20 when you were evangelizing someone with the Gospel? How might you use the verse in its fuller context to help some of your fellow believers who may have backslidden in their faith?

Seeing the Bible Come Alive together! Take time to discuss as a group the following questions.

1. What's your favorite Bible verse?
2. How do you understand or interpret that favorite Bible verse? In other words, what does that verse mean to you?
3. Now read your favorite Bible verse in its total context.
4. Set the contextual boundaries for your favorite Bible verse.
5. How may your previous understanding or interpretation of your favorite Bible verse need to change in light of that verse's overall context?

For further Discussion:

List below some Bible passages that you believe are commonly taken out of context, or are communicated without contextual boundaries.

Seeing the Bible Come Alive
Step 3

In this section we will look at Step 3 to Seeing the Bible Come Alive.

Step 3 to Seeing the Bible Come Alive!

What was God saying through this Bible passage to the original audience?

The Bible was not **initially** written for us—for me or for you.

This statement may be a surprise to you. But it's true. Most of the Bible was written *first* for specific people, in a specific context, in a specific time period in history. For example, King David wrote many of the Old Testament psalms over 3,000 years ago. These psalms meant something to David and the Jewish people living in Israel at that time. In fact, many of these psalms were worship songs. This was long before they were placed in to the book of the Bible called: The Psalms.

It's the same for the New Testament. The words of the apostle Paul to the church in Corinth, for example, were actual letters written by Paul to the Corinthian Christians in the middle of the first century A.D. Paul wrote these letters to a specific church that had some very specific problems to which Paul was responding. We read these letters today in what we know as the 1 Corinthians or 2 Corinthians. However, they were first written over 2,000 years ago!

The truth is: the Bible was written for people living in contexts different from most of us today. This truth is important to understand because it is essential for good Bible interpretation.

That's why Step 3 is so important. **What was God saying through this Bible passage to the original audience?** To answer this question the Bible interpreter looks at the passage in light of its literary form, contextual boundaries and historical setting. By doing these three things the interpreter attempts to figure out, as best he or she can, what the Bible passage meant to its original hearers.

Let the text speak for itself, first!

In Step 3 the interpreter tries to understand what the Bible passage meant back **then**. Here the Bible interpreter attempts to answer the following question:

What message did the original speaker/writer want to communicate to his original hearers/readers?

Here is the time to pray and ask the Holy Spirit for help. The Bible interpreter must pray and ask God to reveal His Truth that He intended to communicate through the original author and audience.

Such a prayer may go something like this:

"God, through the power of your Holy Spirit, please help me understand what You intended in this passage through the original author to the audience."

So after prayer what do we do? In Step 2, we talked about the importance of context and setting contextual boundaries. Let's look again at the two examples that we already looked at to get some more insights into how to answer Step 3.

Two Examples of Step 3

A. **Example #1: *Psalm 50:10***

"For every beast of the forest is mine, the cattle on a thousand hills."

As we discussed in the last step, the direct context of this passage, as seen within the contextual boundaries of Psalm 50, reveals that verse 10 is not a verse about material blessings. Rather it's a verse found in the overall context of obedience or judgment. God owns everything and expects obedience. He is calling His faithful ones to offer true sacrifices of thanksgiving in obedience to His laws. When they do this they will be blessed.

So what was God saying through this Bible passage to the original audience?

Specific answers to this question are sometimes difficult. However, sometimes we do have some clues. Oftentimes these clues can be found in the title that comes before the Psalm, like in Psalm 49 where the title says, "To the choirmaster. A psalm of the sons of Korah," or in Psalm 3: "A psalm of David, when he fled from Absalom his son." When we compare the historical names ("sons of Korah") or historical events ("when David fled from Absalom his son") with other Scripture passages in which these individuals or events are found, we get a better understanding of the original context of the Psalm.

Psalm 50 has one of these clues. The title reads: "A psalm of Asaph." So who is Asaph? Well, after looking at other Scripture passages that talk about Asaph, we discover that Asaph was a descendant of Levi (see *1 Chronicles 6:43*) who was among the men mentioned in the passage below:

> "Whom David put in charge of the service of song in the house of the LORD after the ark rested there. They ministered with song before the tabernacle of the tent of meeting until Solomon built the house of the LORD in Jerusalem" (1 Chronicles 6:31-32).

We can learn more about Asaph in *1 Chronicles 15:17; 16:5-7; 25:2;* and *2 Chronicles 29:30*. However, enough information is given in the above quote to see that the words of Asaph found in Psalm 50 were written during the time of David before the temple had been built. This is the historical context of the original hearers of this psalm. They were the Israelites who were under the rule of one of their greatest kings, David.

Asaph is reminding the Israelites that even in the midst of the greatness of Israel under David, and their blessings from God, they are still dependent upon God. God still owns everything in the world and does not need anything from humans. He is calling His faithful ones in Israel to offer true sacrifices of thanksgiving in obedience to His laws. When they do this they will be blessed.

By learning more about Asaph we learn more about what God was saying through Psalm 50 to the original audience of Israelites back in David's time.

B. **Example #2: *Revelation 3:20***

"Behold, I stand at the door and knock. If anyone hears My voice and opens the door, I will come in to him and eat with him, and he with me."

So what was God saying through this Bible passage to the original audience?

In this Revelation passage, it's easy to discover both who the original audience is, and what God is saying to them. Already we have seen that the contextual boundaries of this *Revelation 3:20* passage directly relate to the words written to the church in Laodicea *(Revelation 3:14-23).* Here, the backsliding Laodicean believers are given hope that if they repent from their apathy they can have fellowship with God restored once again, even the intimacy of table fellowship.

In many cases, like this *Revelation 3:20* passage, discovering what God was saying through the Bible passage to the original audience is not difficult. It's oftentimes found within the contextual boundaries of the passage itself.

Conclusion

God wants us to understand His Word, the Bible. Sometimes, though, we think that it was only written for us and we forget that it was written for somebody else, first. By looking for what a particular Bible passage meant when it was originally spoken or written, we are attempting to let the Bible speak for itself, first. Sometimes understanding what the text meant to its original audience is easy; sometimes it takes a little more effort. Either way, understanding what God was saying to the original audience/listeners is an important step in doing good Bible interpretation as church planters and disciple makers.

You should now have a good idea of how to look for what God was saying to the original author and his audience back then.

This is Step 3 of the **"Seven Steps to Seeing the Bible Come Alive!"**

Review Questions

1. As a pastor or church planter how do you feel when you read that the Bible was not initially written for you?

2. What does the sentence, "Let the text speak for itself, first" mean to you? Discuss together.

3. Why is it important to first understand what God was saying to the original author and his original audience?

Seeing the Bible Come Alive!

1. Remember your favorite Bible verse from the last section? Read it again in context, paying attention to its contextual boundaries.

2. Pray and ask God to reveal to you what He was saying in your favorite Bible verse to the original author and his audience.

3. Using the context of your favorite Bible verse, what was God saying to the original author and his audience?

For further Discussion: Read the book of Galatians and consider the circumstances that caused Paul to write this letter? Can you imagine the situation of the people and the questions they must have been asking Paul?

Seeing the Bible Come Alive
Step 4

Above we looked at Steps 1-3:

1. What kind of literary form is this Bible passage and what are the implications of this?
2. What are the contextual boundaries of the Bible passage?
3. What was God saying through this Bible passage to the original audience back then?

Here, in this section, we will look in more detail at Step 4:

> **Step 4 to Seeing the Bible Come Alive!**
>
> **_What is the general principle that God had in mind through this Bible passage for all peoples and all cultures?_**

Potential problems we sometimes face as Bible interpreters:

Problem #1: <u>The original context is different from our context today:</u> In this situation, it may seem difficult to interpret correctly the original meaning, and how it relates to people today.

Problem #2: <u>The original context is unknown to us</u>: Sometimes, it is difficult to understand what a particular Bible passage meant to either the original speaker/writer or to his original audience.

There are many possible answers to these two problems. Before seeking answers, however, we must pray and ask the

Holy Spirit for help. Ask God to reveal His Truth that He intended to communicate to everyone through the passage.

Such a prayer may go something like this:

"Dear God, through the power of Your Holy Spirit, please help me understand what You intended in this passage for all peoples and all cultures."

After we pray and seek the Holy Spirit's guidance, what do we do with these two problems? Let's look first at Problem #1.

Problem #1: <u>The original context is different from ours today.</u>

We must always remember that even though a human author spoke or wrote the words found in the Bible, God is the ultimate author of it all. **He is the Divine Author**. The Bible was *"breathed out by God" (2 Timothy 3:16)*. As a result, God had a reason to be intimately involved with the very heart and mind of the human speaker or writer. God knew that because of this intimacy His words would be relevant to the people in their original context as well as **for all peoples and all cultures**. This applies to people like us, who are living 2,000, 3,000 or even 4,000 years after the words of the Bible were originally spoken or written. God wants His book to be understood by every generation, by every culture, and by every person!

As a result, it's worthwhile considering the question: "What did God have in mind in this passage for every person in every culture?" We call this looking for the **general principle** of the passage. In other words:

What is the <u>general principle</u> of the Bible passage that the Divine Author (God), intended for every person in every culture?

We must remember, *"all Scripture is profitable" (2 Timothy 3:16).* This means that **every** Bible passage has a general principle that applies to **every person in every culture**. All too often we neglect large portions of the Bible by saying something like this:

"I just don't understand what the original context is, so the passage must not apply to us and our culture today." OR, "I understand the original context, but the passage just doesn't apply to us in our culture today."

By looking for the general principle of each passage we are saying that the Bible relates to every person in every culture today. It is this general principle that can be taught to our people.

We believe that as we study scripture depending upon the guidance of the Holy Spirit we can discover, **in general terms**, what God is trying to say to all peoples and all cultures.

We can understand what the Divine Author intended for everybody.

Of course, the specific details will be worked out differently since we are of different cultures, worldviews, and backgrounds.

Knowing the original context can help us in knowing the general principle. How? Because knowing the original context helps us to set the boundaries of the possibilities of the general principle. The diagram on the next page helps illustrate this connection between original context and general principle. Let's study it in more detail.

The diagram shows that **back then** God, as the Divine Author, gave the information that He wanted to communicate to the original speaker/writer who, then gave that information to his original audience in either spoken or written form.

Knowing the original context of the first hearer/readers is a help to better understand the general principle that God intends **for all peoples and all cultures**. The arrow in the diagram shows how the original context and the general principle are closely linked together.

Take a good look at the following diagram. See how the connection between back then and for all peoples and all cultures works out.

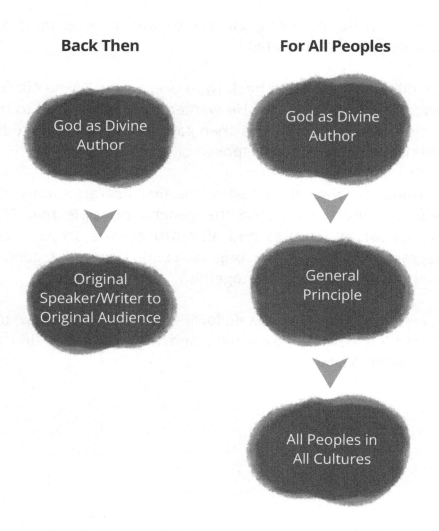

	Back Then	For All Peoples
	God as Divine Author	God as Divine Author
	Original Speaker/Writer to Original Audience	General Principle
		All Peoples in All Cultures

Let's look at two examples of how this general principle works by looking at the two passages we have already examined: *Psalm 50:10* and *Revelation 3:20*.

Two Examples of Step 4

A. **Example #1: _Psalm 50:10_**

"For every beast of the forest is mine, the cattle on a thousand hills."

As we discussed in the last section, in Psalm 50, Asaph is reminding the Israelites that even in the midst of the greatness of Israel under David, and their being blessed by God, they are still dependent upon God. God still owns everything in the world and does not need anything from humans. He is calling His faithful ones in Israel to offer true sacrifices of thanksgiving in obedience to His laws. When they do this they will be blessed.

What is the general principle for all peoples and all cultures? General principles are explained best by using one simple and clear sentence. So the general principle found in Psalm 50:10 is this:

God owns everything and expects obedience.

This general principle comes right out of the original context of *Psalm 50:10* and applies to everyone.

B. **Example #2: *Revelation 3:20***

   "Behold, I stand at the door and knock. If anyone hears my voice and opens the door, I will come in to him and eat with him, and he with me."

As we discussed in the last section, in Revelation 3:20 the backsliding Laodicean believers are given hope that if they repent from their apathy they can have fellowship with God restored once again, even the intimacy of table fellowship.

What is the general principle for all peoples and all cultures? Once again, general principles are explained best using one simple and clear sentence. The general principle found in *Revelation 3:20* is this:

Fellowship with God can be restored for Christians who repent.

Again, this general principle flows directly out of the original context of *Revelation 3:20* and applies to everyone.

Problem #2: <u>The original context is unknown to us.</u>

What do we do if we can't understand what the passage originally meant to the original audience? The key to answering this question is to again look for the general principle that God, the Divine Author, intended everyone to understand. This general principle will not contradict other scripture and will typically be emphasized in other parts of the Bible.

Conclusion

God wants us to understand His Word. Though sometimes the specific details may be unknown, there is still a general principle that God intended for the passage that can be understood by all Christians. In the past, many of us thought that because we couldn't understand a particular Bible passage it was all right to simply skip over it and not apply it to our lives today. Doing good Bible interpretation means that we take the entire Bible seriously. As church planters and disciple makers, we must take the time and effort necessary to understand God's Word—**all** of God's Word.

You should now have a good idea of how to look for the general principle of a passage for all peoples and all cultures. This is Step 4 in the **"Seven Steps to Seeing the Bible Come Alive!"**

Review Questions

1. Have you ever avoided reading parts of the Bible because you didn't understand them? Why?
2. In your own words, describe the phrase: "God as Divine Author."

3. Do you really think that all of the passages found in the Bible have a general meaning for all peoples and cultures today?

4. Why do you think that prayer is so important when trying to find the general meaning of a passage?

Seeing the Bible Come Alive!

1. Remember your favorite Bible verse from the last sections? Read it again in its context, paying attention to its contextual boundaries and what God was saying to the original author and his original audience.

2. Pray and ask God to reveal to you the general principle found in your favorite Bible verse that He intended for all peoples and all cultures.

3. What is the general principle of your favorite passage?

Seeing the Bible Come Alive
Step 5

So far, we looked at Steps 1-4 of the **"Seven Steps to Seeing the Bible Come Alive!"**

1. What kind of literary form is this Bible passage and what are the implications of this?

2. What are the contextual boundaries of the Bible passage?

3. What was God saying through this Bible passage to the original audience back then?

4. What is the general principle that God had in mind through this Bible passage for all peoples and all cultures?

Here we will look in more detail at Step 5:

Step 5 to Seeing the Bible Come Alive!

What is God saying through this Bible passage today?

If the Bible interpretation that you do doesn't impact and change your own life, then it's incomplete, especially in your leadership role as a pastor or church planter. Remember that *"all Scripture...is profitable for teaching, for reproof, for correction, and for training in righteousness."* The truth of *2 Timothy 3:16* applies to the Bible interpreter first. Any Bible passage that we study should **teach <u>us</u>, reprove <u>us</u>, correct <u>us</u>, or train <u>us</u> in righteousness** in some way.

As it's profitable for our own lives, it will help us see how it will also be profitable for the lives of others. Remember, what is true for other people should first be true for us.

The importance of praying and seeking the guidance of the Holy Spirit must be stressed. We are reading God's Word in an attempt to understand what it means for our own life. This is very serious. As a result, we really do need to pray to the Holy Spirit to give us wisdom and insight.

Such a prayer may go something like this:

"Dear God, through the power of your Holy Spirit, please help me understand what you intend for me and my life through this passage."

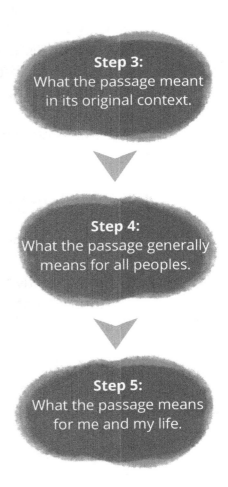

Step 3:
What the passage meant in its original context.

Step 4:
What the passage generally means for all peoples.

Step 5:
What the passage means for me and my life.

After we pray and seek the Holy Spirit's guidance, what do we do next? We look carefully at the work that we have already done in Steps 3 and 4. The relationship between Steps 3, 4, and 5 can be seen in the diagram:

Let's see how Step 5 works by looking back at the two previous passages that we have already worked on: Psalm 50:10 and Revelation 3:20.

Two Examples of Step 5

A. **Example #1: _Psalm 50:10_**

"For every beast of the forest is mine, the cattle on a thousand hills."

Step 3: What the passage meant in its original context:

In Psalm 50, Asaph is reminding the Israelites that even in the midst of the greatness of Israel under David, and their being blessed by God, they are still dependent upon God. God still owns everything in the world and does not need anything from humans. He is calling His faithful ones in Israel to offer true sacrifices of thanksgiving in obedience to His laws and when they do they will be blessed.

Step 4: What the passage generally means for all peoples and all cultures:

God owns everything and expects obedience.

Step 5: What the passage means for me and my life:

Again, Step 5 comes directly from Steps 3 and 4. However, since we are all individuals living in different cultural contexts, our individual relationships with God will be different. As a result, the specific answers that we each give to this question will be answered differently by each one of us. However, the answer still needs to come out of Steps 3 and 4; they cannot stand by themselves without any connection to these two steps.

So, how does this passage impact me and those around me as a member of _____ village, city, state, and country? Some potential examples include:

- Since God owns everything and expects obedience, I need to realize the privilege that it is to serve Him and to do so with humility.
- Since God wants my obedience, I must honestly ask myself in what ways am I truly being obedient to Him; in what ways am I being disobedient?
- In my context, do I depend upon God, myself, or others? How does that impact my obedience to Him?

B. **Example #2: *Revelation 3:20***

"Behold, I stand at the door and knock. If anyone hears My voice and opens the door, I will come in to him and eat with him, and he with Me."

Step 3: What the passage meant in its original context:

In *Revelation 3:20,* the lukewarm Laodicean believers are given hope that if they repent from their backsliding they can have fellowship with God restored once again, even the intimacy of table fellowship.

Step 4: What the passage generally means for all peoples and all cultures:

Fellowship with God can be restored for Christians who repent.

Step 5: What the passage means for me and my life?

Again, Step 5 comes directly from Steps 3 and 4, and our answers to Step 5 will likely be a bit different for each one of us. However, these different answers still need to come from Steps 3 and 4; they cannot stand by themselves without any connection to these two steps.

So, how does this passage impact me and those around me as a member of _____ village, city, state, and country?

- My fellowship with Jesus can be restored once again.
- Jesus is always there-we have to respond. We have to "open the door."
- Intimacy with Jesus is a wonderful thing, like table fellowship.

In summary to all of the above, here's a real truth:

Only when we understand what the passage means for our own life can we go on to Step 6.

We will do that in the next section.

Conclusion

God not only wants us to understand His Word, He wants us to apply it to our own lives. This crucial Step 5 must be done **first** if we are ever going to be authentic to the people that God has called us to disciple. As church planters and disciple makers we must let the Bible speak to us and change our own lives first before we expect the lives of our people to be changed.

You should now have a good idea of how to apply a Bible passage to your own life. This is Step 5 in the **"Seven Steps to Seeing the Bible Come Alive!"**

Review Questions

1. Explain in your own words the relationship between Steps 3, 4, and 5.

2. As a pastor or church planter why do you think that prayer is important when trying to find out what God is saying to you through the passage?

Seeing the Bible Come Alive!

1. Remember your favorite Bible verse from the last section? Read it again in its context, paying attention to its contextual boundaries and what God was saying to the original author and his original audience, as well as to the general principle that He intended for all peoples and cultures.

2. Pray and ask God to reveal what He is trying to say to you through your favorite Bible verse.

3. What is God saying to you today through your favorite Bible verse?

Seeing the Bible Come Alive
Step 6

In Steps 1–5 of the **"Seven Steps to Seeing the Bible Come Alive!"**

1. What kind of literary form is this Bible passage and what are the implications of this?

2. What are the contextual boundaries of the Bible passage?

3. What was God saying through this Bible passage to the original audience back then?

4. What is the general principle that God had in mind through this Bible passage for all peoples and all cultures?

5. What is God saying through this Bible passage today?

Here we will look in more detail at Step 6:

Step 6 to Seeing the Bible Come Alive!

__What is God saying through this Bible passage to your community of believers today?__

Here in Step 6, the Bible interpreter attempts to answer the question: How should the Bible passage be best interpreted for my people today? Above, we talked about how Bible interpretation is best done in community with other believers. You, as a pastor, church planter, or disciple maker, are not learning how to interpret the Bible for yourself, alone.

You are learning to interpret the Bible so that you are better equipped to help your local community of believers—your church or fellowship group that regularly gathers together to learn from God's Word—to better understand the Bible passage and how to apply it to their daily lives. Later in this book we will introduce a few Bible study methods which can help you greatly.

As a disciple maker and church planter, you have a great responsibility to accurately and honestly interpret the Bible. Following the steps outlined in this book can help you. We must also remember to let the Holy Spirit speak through His Word and communicate what He is saying as best you can. **Dependence on the Holy Spirit is the key.**

As a result, at the beginning of Step 6, the Bible interpreter can pray something like this:

"God, through the power of your Holy Spirit, please help me communicate the truths of this Bible passage that you want our community of believers to hear, understand and obey."

The good news here is that if you have done Steps 1 to 5 well, it will not be difficult for you to do Step 6. For, in Step 6, you simply apply the results of Steps 3, 4, and 5 to the local community of believers you are ministering among. The relationship between Steps 3, 4, 5, and 6 is seen in the following diagram that follow:

Once again, let's see how Step 6 works by looking back at the two previous passages that we have already worked on: *Psalm 50:10* and *Revelation 3:20.*

Step 3:
What the passage meant in its original context.

Step 4:
What the passage generally means for all peoples.

Step 5:
What the passage means for me and my life.

Step 6:
What the passage means for my community of believers.

Two Examples of Step 6

A. **Example #1: *Psalm 50:10***

"For every beast of the forest is mine, the cattle on a thousand hills."

Step 3: What the passage meant in its original context:

In Psalm 50, Asaph is reminding the Israelites that even in the midst of the greatness of Israel under David, and their being blessed by God, they are still dependent upon God. God still owns everything in the world and does not need anything from humans. He is calling His faithful ones in Israel to offer true sacrifices of thanksgiving in obedience to His laws and when they do they will be blessed.

Step 4: What the passage generally means for all peoples and all cultures:

God owns everything and expects obedience.

Step 5: What the passage means for me and my life:

- Since God owns everything, I need to realize the privilege that it is to serve Him and to do so with humility.
- Since God wants my obedience, I must honestly ask myself in what ways am I truly being obedient to Him; in what ways am I being disobedient?

Step 6: What the passage means for my community of believers:

Step 6 comes directly from Steps 3, 4, and 5. However, since our communities of believers are living in different cultural contexts, our relationships with God will be different. As a result, the specific answers that we give to this question will be answered differently according to our local context. These specific answers for our communities, however, still need to flow out of Steps 3, 4, and 5; they cannot stand by themselves without any connection to these three steps.

So, how might this passage impact your local community of believers? This should be fairly similar to Step 5:

- Since God owns everything and expects obedience, we need to realize the privilege that it is to serve Him and to do so with humility.
- Since God wants our obedience as His followers, we must honestly ask ourselves in what ways are we truly being obedient to Him; in what ways are we being disobedient?

B. Example #2: *Revelation 3:20*

"Behold, I stand at the door and knock. If anyone hears My voice and opens the door, I will come in to him and eat with him, and he with Me."

Step 3: What the passage meant in its original context:

In *Revelation 3:20,* the backsliding Laodicean believers are given hope that if they repent from their apathy (lack of care) they can have fellowship with God restored once again, even the intimacy of table fellowship.

Step 4: What the passage generally means for all peoples and all cultures:

Fellowship with God can be restored for Christians who repent.

Step 5: What the passage means for me and my life?

- My fellowship with Jesus can be restored once again.
- Jesus is always there-we have to respond. We have to "open the door."
- Intimacy with Jesus is a wonderful thing, like table fellowship.

Step 6: What the passage means for my community of believers:

Our answers to Step 6 will likely be a bit different for each of our communities of believers. However, these different answers still need to flow out of Steps 3, 4, and 5; they cannot be independent or unconnected from the previous steps.

So, how might this passage impact your local community of believers?

- Our fellowship with Jesus can be restored once again.
- Jesus is always there-we are the ones who have to respond. We have to "open the door."
- Intimacy with Jesus is a wonderful thing, like table fellowship.

Conclusion

In summary to all of the above, here's a real truth:

Good Bible interpretation should change both our own lives as well as the lives of our people.

The Bible interpretation that we do should change our lives and the lives of our people. Helping to change lives is a real challenge for all who are church planters and disciple makers. Sometimes such change may occur quickly; at other times change may be slower. The fact remains that the truths of the Bible are for every person who says that he or she is a follower of Jesus. As a pastor or church planter, you are under obligation to interpret the Bible so that lives will be changed. That's what Step 6 is all about.

You should now have a good idea of how to interpret a passage for your community of believers. This is Step 6 in the **"Seven Steps to Seeing the Bible Come Alive!"**

Review Questions
1. Why is it important for a pastor or church planter to accurately and honestly interpret God's Word for his community of believers?

2. Why is knowing the local context of the local body of believers so important for good Bible interpretation?

Seeing the Bible Come Alive!
1. Remember your favorite Bible verse from the last sections? Read it again in its context, paying attention to its contextual boundaries and what God was saying to the original author and his original audience. Also, recall what God spoke to you concerning this passage and your own life.

2. Pray and ask God to reveal to you through your favorite verse what He wants you to communicate to your people so that they will hear, understand and obey His Word.

3. What does God want you to communicate about your favorite verse to your people?

Seeing the Bible Come Alive
Step 7

In Steps 1–6 of the "Seven Steps to Seeing the Bible Come Alive!"

1. What kind of literary form is this Bible passage and what are the implications of this?

2. What are the contextual boundaries of the Bible passage?

3. What was God saying through this Bible passage to the original audience back then?

4. What is the general principle that God had in mind through this Bible passage for all peoples and all cultures?

5. What is God saying through this Bible passage to you today?

6. What is God saying through this Bible passage to your local community of believers today?

Here, we will look in more detail at Step 7:

Step 7 to Seeing the Bible Come Alive!

How will you communicate the truths of this Bible passage to your community of believers?

Let's get to it!

Step 6 deals with the actual truth of the Bible passage and what God is saying to your community of believers through that passage. The emphasis of Step 7 is different. Step 7 is where you try to best **communicate** those truths. You are trying to pass on to your people the truth of the Bible passage as clearly and relevantly as possible, in ways that your people will best understand. Here is where understanding your own local people and their local context is so important.

The difference between Steps 6 and 7 can be thought of both vertically and horizontally. The vertical view shows what God is saying and the horizontal view shows what you are saying. The differences between Steps 6 and 7 are pictured below:

Vertically, what **God** is saying to your community of believers:

God

Community of Believers

Horizontally, what **you** are saying to your community of believers:

You  **Community of Believers**

Here, in Step 7, the Bible interpreter attempts to answer the following two questions about the Bible passage:

- How can the original meaning be best communicated to my people today?
- How can the relevance of the original meaning be told using modern words, terms, means, or ways of understanding?

It's in Step 7 where the Bible interpretation is done at the level of the interpreter and his/her people in their local context. We've already talked about the importance of the Bible context. At the same time, paying attention to the local context of your local community of believers is equally important. Bible interpretation does not occur in a vacuum. In other words, you cannot interpret the Bible without being impacted by the culture and context you live in. If you only rely on your own thought it is possible to misinterpret or misread scripture through western, eastern, or African eyes.

This is why Bible interpretation is done best **in community**, with other believers. All Bible interpretation that is guided by the Holy Spirit should have an effect on the believing community in which the Bible interpretation is occurring, both as individuals and as a group. **This Christian community is the local context.**

This is why it is important that you, as the church planter, understand your community very well. Among some of the questions you should have answers to include:
- Why do they believe the way they do?
- Why do they think the way they do?
- What are their core values?
- What are those things that shape their worldview (the way they think about the world)?
- What kinds of ideas influence them and their decision-making process?

In connection with the actual Bible passage being studied, here are some questions that should be asked in Step 7:

1. How does your local community of believers understand some of the same concepts/ideas/ways of thinking that are found in the particular Bible passage that is being studied?

2. Have there been any recent local events or incidents that have occurred within your community in the recent past (6 months) that might give insights into how they might interpret a particular passage?

3. How will you actually communicate the truths of the Bible passage to your community? What method (movie, TV show, song, indigenous drama or story, and so on) will help explain what the Bible passage is speaking about?

As you can see, there is a lot to Step 7. As a result, at the beginning of Step 7, the Bible interpreter may pray something like this:

"God, through the power of your Holy Spirit, please help me to understand my local community well enough so that I can best communicate the truths of this Bible passage that you want my community of believers to hear, understand and obey."

After prayer, what do we do? Once again, let's see how Step 7 works by looking back at the two previous passages that we have already worked on: *Psalm 50:10* and *Revelation 3:20*. Because we have already studied these passages in depth, we will not go into as much summary detail as we did in previous sections.

Two Examples of Step 7

A. **Example #1: _Psalm 50:10_**

"For every beast of the forest is mine, the cattle on a thousand hills."

Here are some questions that might be good for you to ask yourself regarding the _Psalm 50:10_ passage, your local community of believers in their local context, and Step 7:
- Their understandings of God.
- Their understandings of God's provision for their lives
- Their understandings of possessions

B. **Example #2: _Revelation 3:20_**

"Behold, I stand at the door and knock. If anyone hears My voice and opens the door, I will come in to him and eat with him, and he with Me."

Here are some questions that might be good for you to ask yourself regarding the _Revelation 3:20_ passage, your local community of believers in their local context, and Step 7:

- Their understandings of what fellowship with God means.
- Their understandings of how sin can break that fellowship with God.
- Their understanding of what intimacy with God looks like.
- Their understanding of what repentance is.

Conclusion

It's time to summarize **the "Seven Steps to Seeing the Bible Come Alive!"**

In a very real sense, Steps 1, 2, 3, and 4 are dealing with this:

*What **did** the Biblical text mean **then and there?***

This focuses on strategies that will help you more intelligently **read** the Bible in order to better understand it.

The word, "strategy," just means a plan, approach, or tactic. So, in Steps 1, 2, 3, and 4 we are looking for reading that will better help us understand the Bible. We are looking at how we can better interpret the Biblical text.

Likewise, Steps 5, 6, and 7 are dealing with this:

What does the Biblical text mean here and now?

In Steps 5, 6, and 7 we are trying to discover **Relating Strategies** that will help us more intelligently **relate** the Bible to our local context in order to better understand it. We are looking at how we can better **interpret our local context.**

Developing **both** good reading strategies and good relating strategies are important for all church planters who want to do good Bible interpretation.

We have covered a lot of material concerning the **"Seven Steps to Seeing the Bible Come Alive!"** You have discovered that there is a lot more to good Bible interpretation than you might have at first thought! The good news is that once you get some practice using the "Seven Steps," you will discover they are not as difficult as they may have first appeared to be. As a church planter, you will want to take the time necessary to become more skilled in using the "Seven Steps" so that you will become more effective in your ministry.

Review Questions

1. In your own words, describe the differences between Step 6 and Step 7.

2. As a pastor or church planter, why is knowing how your people think and believe about different issues so important for good Bible interpretation?

3. In your own words, describe the difference between reading strategies and relating strategies.

Seeing the Bible Come Alive!

1. Remember your favorite Bible verse from the last sections? Read it again in its context, paying attention to its contextual boundaries and what God was saying to the original author and his original audience. Also recall what God spoke to you concerning this passage for your own life and for the lives of your people.

2. Pray and ask God to help you understand your local community in your local context well enough so that you can best communicate the truths of your favorite Bible verse in ways that they will hear, understand and obey His Word.

3. How will you communicate the truths of your favorite verse to your people?

Final Thoughts

Here are seven final points to keep in mind as you continue to do Bible interpretation as church planters and disciple makers:

1. **Let the Bible always take priority over the culture**

This means that no matter what we think about the Bible passage, or what our culture thinks, we have to be true to what the Bible alone says. The Bible is always the final authority.

This is sometimes a difficult point for us who are church planters and disciple makers. We desperately want our people to accept the truths found in the Bible. At the same time, these biblical truths often speak against what our people, or their culture thinks. Consequently, we are sometimes tempted to "water down" or dilute the message of the Bible. Resist this temptation!

The truths of the Bible are sometimes not pleasant for us or our people to hear. Nevertheless, we must always obey what the Bible says.

2. **Be humble**

We have been given the tremendous privilege of interpreting the Bible. As a result, we can either be arrogant about this privilege or be humble. Humility and Bible interpretation must go together. As leaders we must be humble both before the biblical text as well as before our community of fellow believers.

3. **Rely on the Holy Spirit and Prayer**

We know that we cannot do good Bible interpretation without lots of reliance upon the Holy Spirit and much prayer. Nothing learned here will be helpful to you unless and until it is bathed in seeking after the Holy Spirit in prayer. *"Pray without ceasing" (1 Thessalonians 5:15).* Good Bible interpretation will always demand this of us.

4. **Teach others how to do good Bible interpretation**

You took this course so that you can now help others to do good Bible interpretation for themselves. This is one of the main points of this course: to help you learn how to better interpret the Bible so that now you, in turn, can help your community of believers, your church, or small group—better understand the Bible and how to apply it to their daily lives.

We believe that this is very much in keeping with the apostle Paul's words to his disciple, Timothy, when he says: *"and what you have heard from me in the presence of many witnesses entrust to faithful men who will be able to teach others also" (2 Timothy 2:2).* In the same way, through this course we have had the privilege to teach you faithful church planters and disciple makers so that you "will be able to teach others also." We all must pass on to others what we have received.

5. **Remember that Bible interpretation Is about making disciples**

Remember, making disciples is what our primary ministry is all about! We want to learn how to better interpret the Bible—and to help others better interpret the Bible—so that we, and they, will become better disciples of Jesus Christ. At its heart, good Bible interpretation is missions: it's helping us, and our people, to become better equipped both to be a disciple as well as to make disciples.

In the midst of our desire to become better interpreters of God's Word we must always keep this in mind. **For if our Bible interpretation does not result in better disciples of Jesus, as well as more disciples of Jesus, then we have missed the mark in our Bible interpretation efforts.**

6. Give yourself the freedom to make mistakes

We all want to interpret the Bible correctly. But sometimes we don't always do this. This is where we need our community of believers, who have also been trained in interpreting God's Word, to help sharpen us as *"iron sharpens iron" (Proverbs 27:17)*. If we have erred in our Bible interpretation, or have let our own view or our culture's view dominate, and we are confronted in this, we need to once again be humble before the Lord and admit our mistake and move on. And we need to have this same attitude towards our people. Our people may make mistakes in their own interpretations. We need to be gentle with them, correct them, and move on.

7. Just do it!

Just do Bible interpretation! It can be done! It's not as difficult as this course may have made it appear. We are confident that, through prayer and the guidance of the Holy Spirit, you will excel in your interpretation of the Bible! **May God continue to use you mightily for His glory as you continue doing Bible interpretation!**

Appendix 1: Literary Forms

Interpreting Story

Everyone enjoys a good story! Did you realize that most of the Bible is filled with stories? Some have estimated about 80 percent of the Bible is story. That means that God likes stories, too! As a disciple maker or church planter, you will need to pay special attention to the stories found in the Bible and how to interpret them.

A story is a "literary form" which simply means a particular style of writing. Sometimes, a story is referred to by the word, "narrative." Most of the Old Testament contains stories. In the New Testament, many stories of Jesus are found in the four Gospels. The book of Acts also contains many stories about the early church. So, let's look at how to interpret stories!

Four Generalizations about Stories

Before we look at how to interpret stories there are four generalizations (or overviews) about the stories found in the Bible to remember:

1. **Stories Honor God:** Stories attempt to honor God. The individual stories of the Bible tell the larger story of God Himself. This larger story shows us what God is like.

2. **Stories Show God's Control:** Stories show God's control over both nature and human life. God is ultimately in control of everything. Both nature and human life are obedient to His will.

3. **Stories Show Important Events:** Stories usually develop from an important event in the life of the individual or the group. The stories that we read in the Bible are there because they were important, either in the life of the particular Bible character, of Israel, or the early church.

4. **Stories Show Good and Bad:** Stories show both the good and the bad of people. Stories do not hesitate to show the negative side of individuals, the nation Israel, or the early church. Stories honestly reveal their characters.

As a result, whenever we look at stories and how to interpret them it's good to remember these four generalizations because they form the overall background to the stories that we find in the Bible.

Analyzing Stories in the Bible

Whenever we examine the stories in the Bible it's good to ask four simple questions:

1. **What was done?** What actually happened in the story? The major events or characters will have the most implications for Bible interpretation.

2. **When or where did it happen?** When or where did the story occur? What are the actual historical events that surround the particular story? These historical events may be in the life of the individual, the group, or both. Where did the actual historical events happen?

3. **Who did the action?** Who are the characters that are taking part in the story? These will include both major and minor characters. The major actors are usually the ones who are

most important to the overall story. Even God can be a major actor in a story.

4. **Why did the characters act the way they did? (Purpose.)** There are actually two parts to the "why" question:

   - Why was the act done in the first place? In other words, why did the major characters act the way they did? What was their motivation or purpose for why they did what they did?
   - Why was the action remembered? Lots of stories happened in the Bible times. Why was this particular story remembered? What is it about this story that was so important that it should be remembered and handed down to future generations?

By asking these four simple questions of what, when, where, who, and why, we will have a good understanding of what the Bible story is all about; especially how it relates to our lives and the lives of our people.

Let's look at a story in the Old Testament and practice interpreting it. We will do this by looking at these four questions in light of the "Seven Steps" as well as what we read in the last chapter concerning "Reading Strategies" and "Relating Strategies."

Let's look at the story found in *2 Samuel 12:1-15*.

Now that you have read this story, consider the Seven Steps and the Reading and Relating Strategies as we examine *2 Samuel 12:1-15.*

Reading Strategies:

Step 1: What kind of literary form is this Bible passage and what are the implications of this?

The literary form found in *2 Samuel 12:1-15a* is story. As a result, we need to look at the questions: What, When, Who, and Why.

Step 2: What are the contextual boundaries of the Bible passage?

In the case of this story in 2 Samuel, the contextual boundaries are from verses 1-15. This is a unit because it begins with Nathan being sent in verse 1 and Nathan returning back to his house in the first sentence of verse 15. Setting the contextual boundaries of stories also helps us as we attempt to answer the What, When, and Who questions.

In the case of *2 Samuel 12:1-15a*:

What? God sends Nathan to tell a story to rebuke David for the sin he has committed against Uriah.

When? After David commits adultery with Bathsheba and kills Uriah her husband.

Who? Major actors: God, Nathan, David, Bathsheba and Uriah.

Minor actors: Rich man with flocks and herds, poor man with one little ewe lamb, poor man's children, traveler, Saul, house of Israel and Judah, Ammonites, David's wives, and the child whom Bathsheba bore.

Most stories will have many major and minor actors. The first thing to do is to try to distinguish the major actors who are most crucial to the overall story from the minor actors who are seemingly less important.

Step 3: What was God saying through this Bible passage to the original audience?

Here is where the first part of the "Why?" question comes into play:

Why was the action done in the first place?

In the case of 2 Samuel 12:1-15, God is sending Nathan to rebuke David for the sin he has committed against Uriah. Here, the previous work we have done helps us to understand this question. What was God saying to the audience?

He was saying that even kings, like David, are not above God's laws.

Step 4: What is the general principle that God had in mind through this Bible passage for all peoples and all cultures?

Here is where the second part of the "Why?" question comes into play:

Why was the story remembered?

In the case of 2 Samuel 12:1-15, the act was remembered so that no future king would think that he was above God's law. But even for peoples and cultures without kings this passage applies. What God has in mind for everyone is this:

No leader or person with power has the right to violate laws and oppress those who have little or no power.

The Reading Strategies that we have looked at above mainly deal with what we can get out of the text itself through using the first four Steps. The Relating Strategies and the last three Steps consider how it works out in our own situations.

Relating Strategies:

Step 5: What is God saying through this Bible passage to you today?

Once again, Step 5 usually flows out of Steps 3, and 4, and oftentimes will be very similar to Step 4. What God is saying to me is this:

When I am in a position of leadership or power in my church, my job, or my work, I have no right to violate human-made or God-made laws. I also cannot take advantage of those under me who have little or no power.

Step 6: What is God saying through this Bible passage to your community of believers today?

Those believers in my church or small group, when in a position of leadership or power—whether in their job or in their work—have no right to violate human-made or God-made laws. They also should not take advantage of those under them who have little or no power.

Step 7: How will you communicate the truths of this Bible passage to your community of believers? In answering this question, it might be helpful to first think about the following questions:

1. In what ways does your community of believers both hear and tell stories? Who are their storytellers?
2. Have there been any recent local events or incidents within your community of believers recently that might relate to this Bible passage? Describe these events and their impact upon the worldview of your community of believers.

3. Are there any stories—especially festivals, music, dramas, ceremonies, dance, and so on—that are already a part of the culture of your community of believers that can be used to relate the truths of this Bible passage?

4. How can you communicate the truths of this Bible passage to your community of believers?

Conclusion

Good job! You are doing Bible interpretation! Now you are learning how to interpret stories. By closely following the Reading Strategies of Steps 1-4 and the Relating Strategies of Steps 5-7 you have been shown how to read and relate stories both for yourself, as a disciple maker and church planter, as well as for your community of believers. You will get a chance to do it yourself in the section below, "Seeing the Bible Come Alive!"

Assignment: Seeing the Bible Come Alive!
1. Read the story found in 2 Samuel 12:15-25.

2. Do Bible interpretation on this story by analyzing it according to the Reading Strategies of Steps 1-4 and the Relating Strategies of Steps 5-7, as found below.

3. Remember to pray through each Step!

Reading Strategies:
<u>Step 1</u>: What kind of literary form is this Bible passage and what are the implications of this?
<u>Step 2</u>: What are the contextual boundaries of the Bible passage?

<u>Step 3</u>: What was God saying through this Bible passage to the original audience?

<u>Step 4</u>: What is the general principle that God had in mind through this Bible passage for all peoples and all cultures?

Relating Strategies:
<u>Step 5</u>: What is God saying through this Bible passage to you today?

<u>Step 6</u>: What is God saying through this Bible passage to your community of believers today?

<u>Step 7</u>: How will you communicate the truths of this Bible passage to your community of believers?

Interpreting Law

There are a lot of law passages in the Old Testament, especially in the books of Exodus, Leviticus, and Deuteronomy. Sometimes when we read these law passages it seems that most of them just don't apply to us today. They seem so old and outdated. That's why the literary form of law is one form that is most neglected by believers today. But as church planters and disciple makers, you know that all Scripture is important for us today, even the law passages. So what's the answer? Here is where we think that Step 4 is so important: looking for the general principle behind the law that God intended for all peoples and all cultures. In this chapter, we will see why this is so. Let's look at how to interpret law!

Background

1. Four General Points about Law

It is important to remember four general points that influence both how the Old Testament law was given, and how we look at Old Testament law today.

- **Law is good:** Oftentimes we think of the Old Testament law as bad or negative. The Israelites saw law as a good thing. As it was originally given, law was not seen as something burdensome. As the Psalmist said, it was a "delight" for them (Psalm 1:2).

- **Law is a voluntary response:** Why did the Israelites delight in the law and want to follow it? Because obeying the law was a chance for them to respond to the gracious act of God in rescuing them from their bondage as slaves in Egypt. As a result, they voluntarily responded to the law because they desired to please this God who had saved them from Egypt.

- **Law helps us know how to respond:** The Israelites not only voluntarily responded to the law, they knew that the law helped them correctly respond both to God and to each other. Before Moses came to them in the middle of their slavery in Egypt, the people didn't know very much about God, and especially how to respond to Him. However, with the giving of the law, they knew in much greater detail how they should respond to their true God, and how they should live their daily lives. Through the law, they also knew how to respond to one another on a daily basis.

- **Law Forms the Nation Israel:** While they were in slavery in Egypt, the Hebrew people were just 12 tribes united by blood ties and their occupation as slaves. Now, with the giving of the law, these different Hebrew peoples became the nation of Israel with their own set of national laws.

It's always good to keep these four points of general background in mind whenever we look at the Old Testament law and how to interpret it.

2. Two Types of Law

Law is fairly easy to interpret when you remember that there are essentially two types of law: universal and situational.

Universal Law: A law that is for all times and all cultures. It's universal and applies to everyone. It's unqualified and unconditional.

The Ten Commandments are examples of universal law.

Interpreting universal law is relatively easy since it applies in the same way, whether in the original context, or for today.

Situational Law: A law that is for a specific situation in a specific culture. It's not universal and does not apply to everyone. It's qualified and conditional. It's dependent on certain circumstances. Sometimes situational law is known as case-by-case law.

Most of the laws found in Exodus, Leviticus and Deuteronomy are examples of situational law.

Interpreting situational law is more complex than universal. This is because the circumstances back then usually were not the same as today. In this case, we need to pay more attention to the general principle of the passage for all peoples and cultures.

Analyzing Situational Law in the Old Testament as seen in Leviticus Chapters 13 and 14

Reading Strategies:

Step 1: What kind of literary form is this Bible passage and what are the implications of this?

The literary form found in Leviticus 13 and 14 is law. Specifically in these two chapters, we find a large section of situational law. This means that we may have to find the general principle that God intended in this passage for all peoples and cultures (Step 4) if we do not have the same situations today.

Step 2: What are the contextual boundaries of the Bible passage?

This section of situational law is found between chapter 12, which deals with the situation of women after childbirth, and chapter 15, which deals with the situations of those who have bodily discharges. In chapters 13 and 14 of Leviticus we find two entire chapters dedicated to laws about impurities like leprosy, or grievous skin diseases, and mildew.

Chapter 13 tells of impurities like skin diseases and mildew that must be corrected before individuals or their possessions are allowed back into the camp.

Chapter 14 tells how to restore those who have become pure through the outlined purification process. These two chapters go together as a contextual unit. They are the contextual boundaries concerning laws relating to skin diseases and mildews.

Step 3: What was God saying through this Bible passage to the original audience?

By reading chapters 13 and 14, we can quickly discern the original context. The Israelites, who Moses is addressing, have a problem with several different types of impurities, especially skin diseases and mildews. The Israelites need to know what to do about these impurities, both in terms of who can remain within the camp (Lev. 13:46) or community of Israelites, as well as to protect that community from possible infectious diseases. They also need to know how restoration happens once these impurities are corrected. As a result, these laws guided Israel back then whenever they encountered impurities like skin diseases and mildews.

Step 4: What is the general principle that God had in mind through this Bible passage for all peoples and all cultures?

While we understand the original context **back then**, it is difficult **for all peoples in all cultures** to relate to it today. As a result, Christians often ignore Leviticus.

By applying Step 4 and the general principle to Leviticus, we can gain many insights from this book for living our Christian lives today. For example, what's the general principle of Leviticus Chapters 13 and 14 **for all peoples and all cultures?**

God has a concern for the welfare of His people, including their health and even their possessions, and He wants to protect them and restore them to fellowship with others.

Relating Strategies:
Step 5: What is God saying through this Bible passage to you today?

Of course, our cultural context is different today: we don't have to go to a priest for physical examination, nor will we be banned from our community because of a medical condition, or for having mildew in our house. At the same time, the general principle of Leviticus still applies.

So what is God saying to me? Based on the general principle, we believe that God is saying that He has a concern for my welfare, including my health and my possessions. He wants to protect me and keep me in fellowship with other believers.

Step 6: What is God saying through this Bible passage to your community of believers today?

Here Steps 4, 5, and 6 will be similar. In my context, Chapters 13 and 14 show us that we, today in our churches, need to remember that God has a very real concern for each one of us and that He wants to protect us from those things that may harm us, both as individuals and as a community of believers. It's also a powerful example of how restoration can occur for those who formerly were harmful to the community.

Step 7: How will you communicate the truths of this Bible passage to your community of believers?

In answering this question, it might be helpful to first think about the following questions:

1. How does your community of believers view situational laws in their own local and national governments that affect their daily lives? Are they positive towards these situational laws, or negative? Do they abide by these situational laws or do they find ways to avoid or get around them?

2. How does your community of believers view situational laws as found in the Old Testament? Do they see any relevancy between biblical situational laws and their own daily lives today?

3. What local events or incidents—in regards to situational law—have occurred within your community of believers in the recent past (6 months) that might give insight into how they interpret situational laws? Describe these events or incidents and their impact upon the worldview of your community of believers.

Conclusion

Good job! You are **doing** Bible interpretation! Now you are learning how to interpret the literary form of law. By closely following the Reading Strategies of Steps 1-4 and the Relating Strategies of Steps 5-7 you have been shown how to read and relate both universal and situational law for yourself as a church planter, as well as for your community of believers. You will get a chance to do it yourself in the section below, "Seeing the Bible Come Alive!"

Review Questions

1. Why is seeing the law as a good thing so important in understanding how law functioned both in the life of Israel as well as in our lives today?

2. What is the difference between universal law and situational law?

3. How does your own community of believers view both universal and situational laws?

Seeing the Bible Come Alive!
Read the situational law passage found in Exodus 21:28-29.
Do Bible interpretation on this law by analyzing this law according to the Reading Strategies of Steps 1-4 and the Relating Strategies of Steps 5-7, as found below.
Remember to pray through each Step!

Reading Strategies:
Step 1: What kind of literary form is this Bible passage and what are the implications of this?

Step 2: What are the contextual boundaries of the Bible passage?

Step 3: What was God saying through this Bible passage to the original audience?

Step 4: What is the general principle that God had in mind through this Bible passage for all peoples and all cultures?

Relating Strategies:
Step 5: What is God saying through this Bible passage to you today?

Step 6: What is God saying through this Bible passage to your community of believers today?

Step 7: How will you communicate the truths of this Bible passage to your community of believers?

Interpreting Poetry

When we think of poetry in the Bible we most often think about entire books that contain poetry, like Psalms and Proverbs, or the prophetic books like Obadiah and Habakkuk. However, poetry is found throughout both the Old and New Testaments in almost every book of the Bible. For example, poetry is found in the songs of Moses and Miriam when rescued from Egypt (Exodus 15), in the prayer of Jonah when he was in the belly of the fish (Jonah 2), in Mary's song of praise (Luke 1), and in the songs of the four living creatures in heaven (Revelation 4 and 5). Poetry is also found throughout books of the New Testament when Jesus and Paul, among others, quote verses from the Old Testament.

Poetry is powerful. The writer of poetry chooses particular words and phrases that have their own way of reaching into the hearts and minds of their readers or listeners. **Poetry is also subtle**. It can cause the hearer to abruptly take notice because of the careful use of a word or phrase. The poetry of the Old Testament, in particular, shows how the Israelites looked at life and how they interpreted the events of life: problems, experiences, beliefs, philosophies, and attitudes. It's no wonder, then, that so much poetry is found throughout the Bible; thus, it's important for church planters and disciple makers to know how to interpret poetry.

It is important to remember that because poetry passages are written to move us and are so expressive emotionally sometimes it is best not to take the verse literally. For example, consider *Psalm 42:1*, where the author states he longs after God like a deer panting for water. We are not to take this to mean that he was actually panting, but that he was earnestly seeking after the Lord. It is likewise with proverbs. A proverb is a generalization that is generally true, although there are exceptions. Consider *Proverbs 15:1*. This statement is generally true but not universally true.

1. Major Types of Hebrew Poetry

There are different kinds of poetry. Some poetry has a **balance of rhyme** between two lines, where the last word in the first line rhymes with the last word in the second line. This is not always easy to see because the Bible was not written in your local language.

Other poetry has a **balance of rhythm or thought**, where the second line is somehow linked to the first line. This second line will affirm the thought in the first line, oppose the thought in the first line, or complete the thought in the first line. Hebrew poetry, as found throughout the Old Testament, has this balance of rhythm. This balance of rhythm between the first line and second line is called "parallelism." Consider the following Example:

"The earth is the Lord's and the fullness thereof, the world and those who dwell therein…" (Psalm 24:1).

"Hear, my son, your father's instruction, and forsake not your mother's teaching" (Proverbs 1:8).

In both of these examples, the second line is basically repeating the same thought as the first line. It just uses different words. In the *Psalms 24:1* example, the "world" and the "earth" are describing the same entity, and the phrase "those who dwell therein" parallels the thought of "the fullness thereof." In the *Proverbs 1:8* example both lines one and two are speaking of obeying ("hear" in line one and "forsake not" in line two) your parent's ("father's" in line one and "mother's" in line two) training ("instruction" in line one and "teaching" in line two). The repetition emphasizes the need for obedience. Consider the following Example:

"For the LORD knows the way of the righteous, but the way of the wicked will perish" (Psalm 1:6).

"A soft answer turns away wrath, but a harsh word stirs up anger" (Proverbs 15:1).

In both of these examples the second line is contrasting what is being said in the first line. Note the use of the key word, "but," in the second lines of both examples.

Consider the following Example:

"And those who know your name put their trust in you, for you, O LORD, have not forsaken those who seek you" (Psalm 9:10).

"The blessing of the LORD makes rich, and he adds no sorrow with it" (Proverbs 10:22).

In both of these examples, the second line completes the first. The first example contains the key word, "for." In the second example, the second line implies the word "because" and the second line cannot stand alone.

Consider the following examples:

"As a deer pants for flowing streams, so pants my soul for you, O God" (Psalm 42:1).

"Iron sharpens iron, and one man sharpens another" (Proverbs 27:17).

In both of these examples, the word picture in the first line illustrates the thought of the second line. The first example contains the key word, "as." In the second example, the key word, "as," is implied in the first line and the word "so" is implied in the second line.

2. **How to Interpret Hebrew Poetry**

There are several general points to consider when interpreting Hebrew poetry, especially in Psalms and Proverbs. Let's look at each one in turn.

- **Determine the Contextual Boundaries:** As we already talked about in Step 2 of the Seven Steps, context is especially important when attempting to interpret poetry. As we have already seen, sometimes in the Psalms there will be titles before the actual text that will help us in terms of who wrote it, why it was written, and what kind of song the poetry represents. This is also true for a few of the Proverbs as well.

- **Understand Parallelism:** So far we have been describing the simplest kind of Hebrew poetry, parallelism. However, there are many other kinds of parallelism, sometimes involving more than two lines, sometimes involving combinations of different kinds of parallelism, and so on. Having said all this, however, simple two-line parallelism is a dominant form found throughout the Old Testament.

- **Remember the many kinds of poetry:** Again, the parallelism of Hebrew poetry is particularly found in the Old Testament. The poetry found in the New Testament does not necessarily follow this kind of parallelism, unless the New Testament writers are using quotations from the Old Testament.

Conclusion

Good job! You are **doing** Bible interpretation! Now you are learning how to interpret the literary form of poetry. By closely following the Reading Strategies of Steps 1-4 and the Relating Strategies of Steps 5-7 you have been shown how to read and relate poetry both for yourself, as well as for your community of believers. You will get a chance to do that yourself in the section below, "Seeing the Bible Come Alive!"

Review Questions
1. Why is it necessary to see that Hebrew poetry is based on a balance of rhythm, also known as parallelism?

2. How does your own community of believers look at the literary form of poetry in their own lives as well as in the Bible?

Seeing the Bible Come Alive!
1. Read the poetry found in *Proverbs 1:8-9*. Pay special attention to the parallelism found in these two verses.

2. Do Bible interpretation on this passage by analyzing this poem according to the Reading Strategies of Steps 1-4 and the Relating Strategies of Steps 5-7, as found below.

3. Remember to pray through each Step!

Reading Strategies:
Step 1: What kind of literary form is this Bible passage and what are the implications of this?

Step 2: What are the contextual boundaries of the Bible passage?

Step 3: What was God saying through this Bible passage to the original audience?

Step 4: What is the general principle that God had in mind through this Bible passage for all peoples and all cultures?

Relating Strategies:
Step 5: What is God saying through this Bible passage to you today?

Step 6: What is God saying through this Bible passage to your community of believers today?

Step 7: How will you communicate the truths of this Bible passage to your community of believers?

Prophecy can be a difficult literary form to interpret. Part of the difficulty lies in the fact that there is much debate about prophets and prophecy today, as well as the fact that false prophets arise from time to time. These facts impact how we look at prophecy in the Bible. But we need to understand prophecy and how it functions in Scripture since prophecy is found throughout the Bible. Prophecy is found in the books of the Old Testament known as the four major (longer writings) prophets: Isaiah, Jeremiah, Ezekiel and Daniel. Prophecy is also found in the books of the Old Testament known as the 12 minor (shorter writings) prophets: Hosea, Joel, Amos, among others. Prophecy is also found in the New Testament with individuals who are called prophets—as well as prophecy in the early church being a specific spiritual gift.

So, how will we approach the literary form of prophecy? We will approach it from the standpoint of how to interpret it as a literary form. We will not be concerned about whether or not there are prophets today, or mapping future events according to prophecies, nor will we be concerned about questions related to the spiritual gift of prophecy. Though these topics are important, they do not help us much in trying to interpret prophecy that we find in the Bible. As a disciple maker and church planter, it's important for you to know how to interpret this literary form since it often is a very interesting topic for your community of believers.

1. **Four General Points about Prophecy**

   - **The Definition of a Prophet:** A prophet is a spokesperson for God who declares God's will to the people. The emphasis is on the *message* of the prophet.

- **The Historical Setting of the Prophet:** The prophets spoke their messages in certain specific historical settings. Therefore, we can only properly understand the message of the prophets by first understanding the historical situation in which the prophet preached his message.

- **The Life Situation of the Prophet:** The prophet's own life situation was often intimately linked with his message (for example, Hosea and his marriage to a prostitute as a representation of Israel's relationship with God). As a result, the Bible interpreter must pay close attention to both the various incidents in the prophet's life, as well as the personal experiences that the prophet has with God.

- **The Message of the Prophet:** The message of the prophet was initially delivered orally. It was spoken and/or preached to the people. These short speeches or utterances are called "oracles." The message of any oracle begins with God. The prophet then communicates what God says using his own words in ways that the people can understand. Oftentimes, these oracles are preached in poetic form and are very similar to other Hebrew poetry.

It's important to remember that the prophecy you are reading was not originally intended for you. As a result, the specific issues that the prophet deals with in his message are usually not your specific issues or those of your local community of believers.

As a result, whenever we look at prophecy and how it's interpreted, it's good to keep these four general points in mind.

They form the background to the prophecy that we find throughout the Bible.

2. **Two Types of Prophecy**

Prophecy is fairly easy to interpret when you remember that prophecy involves **both** forthtelling and foretelling.

Forthtelling: Prophecy as *forthtelling* is primarily exhorting the people. It's calling the people to repentance from their disobedience, or from their doubting. Forthtelling is also giving the people God's blessing. Most prophecy falls into the category of forthtelling.

Forthtelling always has a **present aspect**. It relates to the people in their present circumstances.

Foretelling: Prophecy as foretelling is predictive. The prophet announces the future as part of his message of doom or deliverance. However, such foretelling is rooted in the present situation of the people. Furthermore, it always comes out of the forth-telling exhortation. Not all prophecy is foretelling.

Foretelling always has a **future aspect**. It relates to something that will happen in the future as a result of the present situation of the people.

Interpreting prophecy as forthtelling and/or foretelling is sometimes difficult for today. This is because of the dual nature of prophecy as both forthtelling, and foretelling. It's also because any foretelling is rooted in forthtelling; it always has something to do with the present situation of the people. Since the situations back then usually are not the same situations of today, we need to pay more attention to the general principle of the passage for all peoples and cultures. It is an easy temptation to try and apply all prophetic passages to events in our current day. This is a mistake many interpreters have made down through the centuries, sometimes with disastrous results.

Let's now look at a specific example of how to interpret prophecy by looking at prophecies of the prophet Isaiah, found in *Isaiah 7:10-17*.

Analyzing Prophecy: An Example from *Isaiah 7:10-17*

We will walk you through the Seven Steps and the Reading and Relating Strategies in order as we examine the verses found in *Isaiah 7:10-17*.

Reading Strategies:

Step 1: What kind of literary form is this Bible passage and what are the implications?

The literary form found in *Isaiah 7:10-17* is prophecy. As a result, the situation that the prophet Isaiah is addressing to King Ahaz may or may not be our same situation. We may need to look for the general principle of the verses in order for the passage to have meaning for us today.

Step 2: What are the contextual boundaries of the Bible passage?

Isaiah 7:10-17 is found in the overall context of *Isaiah 7:1-8:4*. Here, the historical context is that Syria and the northern kingdom of Israel have united against the southern kingdom of Judah and Jerusalem, ruled by King Ahaz. King Ahaz is afraid *(Isaiah 7:1-2)*. The prophet Isaiah is sent to comfort Ahaz *(Isaiah 7:3)* and, through forthtelling, he exhorts him not to fear. In the midst of this forthtelling, he foretells that this alliance between Syria and Israel will be destroyed. Isaiah encourages Ahaz to stay firm in his faith in God *(Isaiah 7:4-9)*.

Isaiah 7:10-17 follows. Here, God, in order to convince Ahaz, tells him to ask for a sign that what Isaiah says will be true. Ahaz refuses *(Isaiah 7:10-12)*. The prophet Isaiah then says that God will indeed give Ahaz a sign *(Isaiah 7:13)*, forthtelling that God will be with him when "The virgin shall conceive and bear a son, and shall call his name Immanuel" *(Isaiah 7:14)*. A son will be born at that time and before he is old enough to make decisions the two kings threatening Judah will be destroyed by Assyria *(Isaiah 7:15-17)*.

Though the thought of *Isaiah 7:10-17* continues on throughout verses 18-25, these following verses are basically all referring to the same impending fact: Assyria will destroy Syria and the northern kingdom (Israel) and Judah will be blessed. As a result, *Isaiah 7:10-17* should be seen as a unit complete in itself, with *Isaiah 7:1-9* setting the stage, and *Isaiah 7:18-25* following up with what will happen.

Step 3: What was God saying through this Bible passage to the original audience?

God, through the prophet Isaiah, is telling King Ahaz (and the people of Judah) not to fear the historical events that are occurring, namely the political alliance of Syria and Israel. This is the exhortation: "Don't fear, God will take care of you". Out of this prior forthtelling, the foretelling comes: "God will give Ahaz a sign. In the near future a child will be born to the virgin and his name will be Immanuel, 'God with us,' showing Ahaz and the people of Judah that God is indeed with them." This foretelling was fulfilled with the birth of a son to the virgin

(Isaiah 8:3-4). Within two years Syria and the northern kingdom were destroyed by Assyria.

Of course, in the New Testament, Matthew uses the promise of *Isaiah 7:14* to foretell the birth of the ultimate Immanuel, Jesus Himself *(Matthew 1:23)*. While the foretelling of *Isaiah 7:14* is ultimately referring to Jesus, it was also first fulfilled for both Isaiah and Ahaz with the arrival of Assyria and the defeat of the two kingdoms. While Matthew correctly uses *Isaiah 7:14* as a proof-text for the foretelling of the supernatural birth of Jesus, neither Isaiah nor Ahaz had any knowledge of this second and messianic foretelling that was to happen much further in the future. God, of course, knew all of this! He was the One who prompted Matthew to quote *Isaiah 7:14* in relationship to the birth of His Son.

Isaiah 7:14 is thus another good reminder to us to be careful to always let the text speak for itself, first.

Step 4: What is the general principle that God had in mind through this Bible passage for all peoples and all cultures?

The general principle here is a bit more complicated because of both elements of forthtelling and foretelling, as well as the near and far nature of the foretelling. Simply put, the general principle is this:

In times of trouble God is always in control of history and His followers who obey Him do not need to fear. God is with them. This promise is especially seen in His Son, Jesus Christ.

Relating Strategies:

Step 5: What is God saying through this Bible passage to you today?

For me today, as a follower of Jesus, I need to recognize that in times of trouble in my life God is in control and I need not fear. He is with me, especially through His Son, Jesus Christ.

Step 6: What is God saying through this Bible passage to your community of believers today?

One may view it as primarily foretelling the birth of Jesus. They would not see that the passage, and especially verse 14, had an original purpose for the original audience back in Isaiah's day. My community would have to be shown how Step 6 flows out of Steps 4, and 5. They would have to be shown that the passage originally meant something first to Ahaz and the people of Judah. Once they understood this fact, then *Isaiah 7:10-17* would remind my community of believers that God is in control even in times of trouble and that we need not fear. God is with us, especially through His Son, Jesus Christ.

Step 7: How will you communicate the truths of this Bible passage to your community of believers?

In answering this question, it might be helpful to first think about the following questions in relationship to prophecy:

1. What attitudes do your community of believers have towards prophets and prophecy today? How do they view someone today who is considered a prophet? Are they positive or negative towards prophets? Are these prophets within their community or outside? What is their response when the prophet is incorrect?

2. Does your community of believers understand prophecy as forthtelling (exhortation), or foretelling (prediction), or both? What attitudes do your community have towards the

prophets and prophecies (both forthtelling and foretelling) that are found in the Bible?

3. If they occur, in what ways are modern-day prophecies, or prophetic utterances, communicated in your community of believers? Is it through word of mouth, texting, tabloids, radio, TV? How do they view these prophecies in relationship to their own daily lives?

4. What local events or incidents—in regards to prophets and/or prophecies—have occurred within your community of believers in the recent past (6 months) that may give insight into how they interpret prophecy? Describe these events or incidents and their impact upon the worldview of your community of believers.

Conclusion

Good job! You are **doing** Bible interpretation! Now you know how to interpret the literary form of prophecy. By closely following the Reading Strategies of Steps 1-4 and the Relating Strategies of Steps 5-7 you have been shown how to read and relate letters both for yourself, as well as for your community of believers. You will get a chance to do that yourself in the section below, "Seeing the Bible Come Alive!"

Review Questions

1. Why is it so important to see that prophecy is either forthtelling or foretelling? Why does foretelling always come out of forthtelling?

2. Why is understanding the historical context of the prophet and his prophecy so important to a correct interpretation?

3. How does your own community of believers look at the literary form of prophecy in their own lives as well as in the Bible?

Seeing the Bible Come Alive!

1. Read the story of the prophet Jonah in *Jonah 3:1-10*. Pay special attention to the prophetic words that God spoke through Jonah to the people of Nineveh in verse 4.

2. Do Bible interpretation on this passage by analyzing this prophecy according to the Reading Strategies of Steps 1-4 and the Relating Strategies of Steps 5-7, as found below.

3. Remember o pray through each Step!

Reading Strategies:

Step 1: What kind of literary form is this Bible passage and what are the implications of this?

Step 2: What are the contextual boundaries of the Bible passage?

Step 3: What was God saying through this Bible passage to the original audience?

Step 4: What is the general principle that God had in mind through this Bible passage for all peoples and all cultures?

Relating Strategies:

Step 5: What is God saying through this Bible passage to you today?

Step 6: What is God saying through this Bible passage to your community of believers today?

Step 7: How will you communicate the truths of this Bible passage to your community of believers?

Jesus was a master teacher: He knew how to communicate his messages in such a way that young and old, rich and poor, highly educated Pharisees and common people without education, all could understand him. He communicated with such skill and authority that on more than one occasion people who heard him "were astonished at his teaching" *(Matthew 7:28)*, and some even questioned where he got his learning: "How is it that this man has learning, when he has never studied?" *(John 7:15)*.

Jesus was a master storyteller: He never tired of confronting the Jewish religious leaders with an insightful story or an appropriate counter question to their many questions. The crowds loved sitting and listening to Jesus speak for hours at a time. And they remembered what he said. The sayings of Jesus (as well as the teachings and events in the life of Jesus) were compiled and written down by the four Gospel writers: Matthew, Mark, Luke, and John.

As a master teacher Jesus used many different ways to communicate his sayings and teachings. One major way that Jesus communicated was through using figures of speech. A figure of speech is a way to say something in a figurative or nonliteral sense. It's a way to communicate a message in a distinctive way so that it's remembered more easily.

The Sayings of Jesus and Figures of Speech

There are many different figures of speech that Jesus used.

Exaggeration: Exaggeration is an overstating of the obvious; saying more than what is really meant, to make a point. Here are some examples of Jesus' use of exaggeration:

"Why do you see the speck that is in your brother's eye, but do not notice the log that is in your own eye? Or how can you say to your brother, 'Let me take the speck out of your eye,' when there is the log in your own eye? You hypocrite, first take the log out of your own eye, and then you will see clearly to take the speck out of your brother's eye" (Matthew 7:3-5).

Jesus' use of exaggeration is clearly evident: a person cannot physically have a log in his/her eye. Jesus is exaggerating to make his point. His exaggeration is not to be taken literally. Jesus is not really speaking about specks, eyes and logs at all. Rather, he is making the point for us not to be so quick to see fault with somebody else and not see that we also have big faults in our own lives. The overall context of *Matthew 7:1-5* makes his point clear.

Hyperbole: Hyperbole is a deliberate extreme overstatement and excessive exaggeration to make a point. Here's an example of Jesus' use of hyperbole:

"If your right eye causes you to sin, tear it out and throw it away. For it is better that you lose one of your members than that your whole body be thrown into hell. And if your right hand causes you to sin, cut it off and throw it away. For it is better that you lose one of your members than that your whole body go into hell" (Matthew 5:29-30).

Jesus' use of hyperbole is clearly evident: people are not being encouraged to literally tear out their right eyes or cut off their right hands so that they do not sin. Jesus is using excessive exaggeration to make his point. His hyperbole is not to be taken literally.

In the *Matthew 5:29-30* example, Jesus is not really speaking about tearing out right eyes and cutting off right hands. Rather, he is making a point about the seriousness of sin in our lives and the fact that we need to do something about that sin since it can indeed ultimately lead to hell. The overall context of *Matthew 5:29-30* (and the greater context of *Matthew 5:21-48)* makes his point clear. Individuals in Jesus' day were thinking that if they simply kept the letter of the law they were without sin; in this case, if they did not commit the actual act of adultery, they were not sinners, no matter what they thought about a woman in their heart. Jesus, through his use of hyperbole, shows them the futility of their thinking: that if they even looked at a woman lustfully, they had sinned.

Counter Question: Counter question is a method of arguing, where a question is used to answer a previous question or reply. Jesus especially enjoyed using counter question when the Jewish religious leaders asked him a question.

> *"And a man was there with a withered hand. And they asked him, 'Is it lawful to heal on the Sabbath?'—so that they might accuse him. He said to them, 'Which one of you who has a sheep, if it falls into a pit on the Sabbath, will not take hold of it and lift it out'" (Matthew 12:11-12).*

Jesus answers the one asking the question with his own question. In the *Matthew 12:1-2* example, the overall context of *Matthew 12:9-14* makes clear that Jesus wants the religious leaders to think more deeply about law, Sabbath, and helping human beings, and his counter question is followed up by his healing of the man with the withered hand.

Proverb: A proverb is a short compact saying that contains a truth that is worth remembering. When Jesus speaks a proverb we do not know if he is quoting an already well-known proverb or if he is making up his own. Either way, the point is to try to understand the truth in the proverb that is worth remembering.

"And when Jesus heard it, he said to them, 'Those who are well have no need of a physician, but those who are sick. I came not to call the righteous, but sinners'" (Mark 2:17).

"Jesus said to him, 'No one who puts his hand to the plow and looks back is fit for the kingdom of God'" (Luke 9:62).

In both of these examples, we do not know if Jesus is quoting from an already known proverb, or is making up his own proverb to fit the situation. In the *Mark 2:17* example, the overall context is *Mark 2:15-17*, showing Jesus eating with "tax collectors and sinners" (verse 15), much to the frustration of the religious leaders who ask his disciples why he eats with such individuals (verse 16). Jesus' reply is in two parts. In the first part he tells the proverb: "Those who are well have no need of a physician, but those who are sick" (verse 17a). In the second part he comments on the proverb: "I came not to call the righteous, but sinners" (verse 17b). In this case his comments on the proverb explain the proverb's point.

In the *Luke 9:62* example, Jesus gives the proverb without comment. The overall context is the cost involved in following Jesus *(Luke 9:57-62)*, of which this proverb forms the conclusion. The point of the proverb is seen in this overall context: if anyone wants to follow Jesus he/she cannot be distracted by the things of this world; the kingdom of God must have priority.

Three General Points about Interpreting the Sayings of Jesus

There are three general points to consider when interpreting the sayings of Jesus. Let's look at each one in turn.

1. **Figures of speech are universal:** The beauty of Jesus' use of figures of speech is that the majority of cultures and languages today still use figures of speech. Think of the many figures of speech that your own language uses. This is one of the reasons why the words of Jesus are so easy to understand (but not always so easy to obey!).

2. **Determine the type of figure of speech being used:** So, we have looked at some of the major types of figures of speech that Jesus uses. There are others, and your own familiarity with how language works in your own culture will help you identify these others as well. Again, knowing the kind of figure of speech that Jesus is using in a particular saying will go a long ways in helping you understand and interpret what Jesus is saying.

3. **Determine the contextual boundaries:** As we already talked about in Step 2 of the Seven Steps, context is especially important when attempting to interpret the sayings of Jesus and the figures of speech that he uses. As we have already seen in in this chapter, **every** figure of speech must be seen in its overall context. What the figure of speech really means can only be understood in its overall context.

Conclusion
Good job! You are **doing** Bible interpretation! Now you are learning how to interpret the sayings of Jesus. By closely following the Reading Strategies of Steps 1-4 and the Relating

Strategies of Steps 5-7 you have been shown how to read and relate the sayings of Jesus both for yourself, and for your community of believers. You will get a chance to do that yourself in the section below, "Seeing the Bible Come Alive!"

Review Questions

1. Why is knowing that Jesus was a master teacher in his own time helpful for understanding Jesus in your own time period?

2. Why is understanding the various types of figures of speech helpful to us as we interpret the sayings of Jesus?

3. How does your own community of believers look at figures of speech in their own lives as well as in the Bible?

Seeing the Bible Come Alive!

1. Read again the sayings of Jesus found in Matthew 7:3-5 that we already studied above. Pay special attention to the figures of speech that Jesus is using.

2. Do Bible interpretation on this passage by analyzing these sayings of Jesus according to the Reading Strategies of Steps 1-4 and the Relating Strategies of Steps 5-7, as found below. Remember to pray through each Step!

Reading Strategies:

Step 1: What kind of literary form is this Bible passage and what are the implications of this?

Step 2: What are the contextual boundaries of the Bible passage?

Step 3: What was God saying through this Bible passage to the original audience?

<u>Step 4</u>: What is the general principle that God had in mind through this Bible passage for all peoples and all cultures?

Relating Strategies:
<u>Step 5</u>: What is God saying through this Bible passage to you today?

<u>Step 6</u>: What is God saying through this Bible passage to your community of believers today?

<u>Step 7</u>: How will you communicate the truths of this Bible passage to your community of believers?

The Parables of Jesus

As we previously saw, Jesus was a master teacher. One of his most well-known and effective ways of communicating was through parables. Jesus told parables to all kinds of people: his disciples, the religious leaders of the day, and crowds of regular people. And the crowds loved him. But why did Jesus teach in parables?

Jesus taught in parables because everybody enjoys a good story. At its heart, a parable is simply a story. But it's much more than just a story. A parable is a story that's trying to make a point. That's what the very word "parable" means: a story that's making its point through a comparison. In many ways, a parable is just an extended, or longer, simile—similar to those that we studied in the previous chapter. Lots of Jesus' public teaching was through parables. As a result, it's important for church planters and disciple makers to know how to interpret Jesus' parables.

Background: Five Points about Parables

1. **Parables come from the everyday lives of the people:** The material for Jesus' parables came from the daily life of those who were hearing the parables. Most everyone could relate to looking for a lost coin, or to the events surrounding a wedding, or to sowing seed in a field, or to dishonest managers. Jesus used examples from everyday life. That's one reason why his parables were so popular with the people.

2. **Look for the main point:** As we already read above, a parable is a story that is trying to make a point. As a result, it is important for those of us who are trying to interpret the parable to look for the main point. Sometimes this main point of comparison is very easy to find, especially when Jesus talks about the Kingdom of God. At other times, it is more difficult.

3. **The details are not important:** While the main point of a parable is important, the specific details found within a parable are usually not important. Sometimes interpreters will get too concerned about the many details of a parable; they will try to give a spiritual or deeper meaning to the characters and events in the parable.

4. **Understand the purpose of the parable for both Jesus and the Gospel writer:** When we interpret the parables of Jesus, we more accurately interpret them by looking at both what Jesus had in mind for his original audience when he originally spoke the parable, as well as by looking at what the Gospel writer had in mind when he remembered and/or recorded the parable for his audience. In other words, Jesus had a reason why he spoke the parable to his original

audience, and the Gospel writer had a reason for why he remembered and/or recorded the parable for his audience.

5. **Parables are stories:** Since parables are stories, it is helpful to treat them in the same way that we learned how to interpret stories back in Chapter 8. Consequently, with parables, it is also helpful to look at the What, When, Where, Who, and Why questions that will help us better understand the parable. This is especially important in Steps 2, 3, and 4 of the Seven Steps.

As a result, whenever we look at parables and how to interpret them, it's good to keep these five general points in mind.

Conclusion

Good job! You are beginning **to do** Bible interpretation! Now you are learning how to interpret the literary form of parable. By closely following the Reading Strategies of Steps 1-4 and the Relating Strategies of Steps 5-7 you have been shown how to read and relate parables. You will get a chance to do it yourself in the section below, "Seeing the Bible Come Alive!"

Review Questions

1. Why is it important to look for the main point of a parable and not get distracted by all the details that might also be found in the parable?

2. Why is it necessary to look at how the Gospel writer used the parable for his own audience?

3. How does your own community of believers hear and tell parables?

Seeing the Bible Come Alive!

1. Read the parable found in *Matthew 25:1-13.*

2. Do Bible interpretation on this parable by analyzing it according to the Reading Strategies of Steps 1-4 and the Relating Strategies of Steps 5-7, as found below. Be careful not to allegorize the parable.

3. Remember to pray through each Step!

Reading Strategies:

<u>Step 1</u>: What kind of literary form is this Bible passage and what are the implications of this?

<u>Step 2</u>: What are the contextual boundaries of the Bible passage?

<u>Step 3</u>: What was God saying through this Bible passage to the original audience?

<u>Step 4</u>: What is the general principle that God had in mind through this Bible passage for all peoples and all cultures?

Relating Strategies:

<u>Step 5</u>: What is God saying through this Bible passage to you today?

<u>Step 6</u>: What is God saying through this Bible passage to your community of believers today?

<u>Step 7</u>: How will you communicate the truths of this Bible passage to your community of believers?

Letters produce different responses in different people. Some look upon letters in a positive way: they enjoy receiving long hand-written letters from friends and loved ones. Increasingly around the world today, emails, texts, and Facebook are replacing letters. It's important for you to know how your community of believers looks at letters.

A letter is, once again, one of many literary forms. The second half of the New Testament is filled with letters, sometimes called "epistles." These letters were written mainly by the Apostle Paul, and also by John, Peter, and James. Most of these letters were written on specific occasions to specific audiences in various parts of Asia Minor where congregations of the early church were found: Rome, Corinth, Ephesus, Galatia, and so on.

Background: Four Points to Keep in Mind

Before we look at how to interpret letters, there are four general points to keep in mind:

1. **Only in the New Testament:** The literary form of letter is found only in the New Testament.

2. **They were not for you directly:** You are reading somebody else's letter! The particular New Testament letter you are reading was not originally intended for you. As a result, the specific issues that the letter deals with are usually not your specific issues or those of your local community of believers.

3. **Original context is sometimes difficult:** The New Testament letters were written almost 2,000 years ago so

it's sometimes difficult to understand what the specific issues originally were.

4. **Danger of proof-texting:** Sometimes we use a sentence or phrase in a letter to support our own particular viewpoints or to promote our own specific agendas. This is "proof-texting." It's usually not a good practice for those who desire to be good Bible interpreters.

As a result, whenever we look at letters and how to interpret them, it's good to keep these four general points in mind. They form the background to the letters that we find in the New Testament.

Conclusion
Good job! You are doing Bible interpretation! Now you are learning how to interpret the literary form of letter. By closely following the Reading Strategies of Steps 1-4 and the Relating Strategies of Steps 5-7 you have been shown how to read and relate letters. You will get a chance to do that yourself in the section below, "Seeing the Bible Come Alive!"

Review Questions
1. Why is setting the contextual boundaries so important with the literary form of letter?

2. How do you feel about the fact that the particular New Testament letter you are reading was not originally intended for you?

3. How does your own community of believers look at the literary form of letters in their own lives as well as in the New Testament?

Seeing the Bible Come Alive!

1. Read the words that Paul speaks to children and parents in his letter to the church at Ephesus found in *Ephesians 6:1-4.*

2. Do Bible interpretation on this letter by analyzing this passage according to the Reading Strategies of Steps 1-4 and the Relating Strategies of Steps 5-7, as found below.

3. Remember to pray through each Step!

Reading Strategies:

Step 1: What kind of literary form is this Bible passage and what are the implications of this?

Step 2: What are the contextual boundaries of the Bible passage?

Step 3: What was God saying through this Bible passage to the original audience?

Step 4: What is the general principle that God had in mind through this Bible passage for all peoples and all cultures?

Relating Strategies:

Step 5: What is God saying through this Bible passage to you today?

Step 6: What is God saying through this Bible passage to your community of believers today?

Step 7: How will you communicate the truths of this Bible passage to your community of believers?

Revelation refers both to the last book in the New Testament, as well as to a literary form known as "apocalyptic." Apocalyptic literature is a revealing literature: it reveals, or discloses, or makes known, especially about those events that will happen at the end of time. The writer of apocalyptic literature is trying to reveal that which is has not yet been revealed.

Apocalyptic as a literary form is found in the Old Testament in parts of the books of Ezekiel, Daniel, Zechariah, and Isaiah. In the New Testament it is found primarily in Revelation.

The literary form of apocalyptic is usually difficult to interpret. Lots of Christians love to try to "figure out" the rich imagery and symbolic language found in the book of Revelation, and sometimes they come up with some very elaborate interpretations! This is why it is important for disciple makers and church planters to know how to interpret apocalyptic literature in general, and the book of Revelation in particular.

Background to Apocalyptic Literature in General

Before we look at how to interpret the book of Revelation, there are four general points to keep in mind concerning apocalyptic literature:

1. **Apocalyptic looks to the end of history:** The writers of apocalyptic literature have one purpose: to tell their audience about the end times. In other words, the writers are concerned about what's going to happen at the very end of history. It is future-oriented.

2. **Apocalyptic doesn't care about details and precise timelines:** As was true with parables so too with

apocalyptic literature: the details and the timelines are not what's important. Rather, the importance is found in the overall fact that everything that is being talked about refers to the writer's understanding of the end of history. As a result, we need to be very careful about not reading too much into either the details or the timelines. The most important thing to remember is that the writer is trying to make some point about the end of history.

3. **Apocalyptic is formally stylized with vivid images:** In apocalyptic literature, both time and events are talked about in nice neat packages, often with the symbolic use of numbers. Apocalyptic also consists of vivid and sometimes bizarre images of dreams and visions, with hidden meanings and symbols. **In many cases these images are not to be understood literally.** Again, the writers of apocalyptic are not concerned about the details. They are concerned about making a point about the end of history.

4. **Apocalyptic can lead to proof-texting:** Sometimes we use a sentence or phrase from the book of Revelation to back up our own viewpoint, or to promote our own specific opinion, especially about the end of history. Again, this is "proof-texting," and is not a good practice for those who desire to be good Bible interpreters.

Book of Revelation

There are also four general points to keep in mind when interpreting the book of Revelation:

1. **Author:** Most Bible scholars agree that the introduction at the very beginning of the book, "The Revelation to John," indicates John, "the beloved disciple" of Jesus, as the human author. John is thought to have written the gospel of John,

as well as the three letters in the New Testament that also bear his name. John was very old when he wrote Revelation.

2. **Revelation is a letter:** John writes the book of Revelation as a letter "to the seven churches that are in Asia" *(Revelation 1:4).* As a result, all of the apocalyptic elements of Revelation must be seen in the overall context of the letter. John tells about the purpose of his letter to these seven churches: "to show his servants the things that must soon take place" *(Revelation 1:1; also 22:6).* John is using the literary form of apocalyptic to show these churches what the future will soon be. This is the specific occasion or reason for Revelation.

3. **Revelation contains prophecy:** From the very beginning of his letter, John makes clear that his letter is also prophecy: "Blessed is the one who reads aloud the words of this prophecy..." *(Revelation 1:3).* At the very end of the letter, John once again repeats the fact that it is prophecy: "Blessed is the one who keeps the words of the prophecy of this book" *(Revelation 22:7).* Since the prophecy found in Revelation is contained in the literary form of apocalyptic, any prophecy will be directed towards what's going to be happening at the end of history. As we already learned, prophecy has elements of both forthtelling (exhortation) and foretelling (predictions of the future). Many who attempt to interpret Revelation forget these two elements of prophecy. As a result, they primarily stress the foretelling elements.

4. **John's concern:** John, when writing Revelation, has suffered persecution at the hands of the Roman government and has been banished to the island of Patmos. Those in the seven churches have also suffered from persecution.

John is encouraging the believers in the seven churches to persevere in the midst of the persecution. He is also showing them that God's wrath or judgment will soon fall on the persecutors themselves. Furthermore, through the apocalyptic imagery, **John is showing that God is in control of history** and those who are persecuted will indeed triumph in the end times if they remain faithful. John is showing the seven churches "what must soon take place" *(Revelation 22:6)* and to remind them that no matter what, Jesus is "coming soon" *(Revelation 22:7)*. **This is good news: there is hope for all believers who remain faithful to the end.**

Whenever we look at apocalyptic literature, and especially the book of Revelation, it's good to keep all of the above background points in mind. Doing so will help us be better interpreters of apocalyptic literature in general, and the book of Revelation in particular.

Conclusion

Good job! You are **doing** Bible interpretation! Now you are learning how to interpret the literary form of apocalyptic, especially with the book of Revelation. By closely following the Reading Strategies of Steps 1-4 and the Relating Strategies of Steps 5-7 you have been shown how to read and relate Revelation. You will get a chance to do that yourself in the section below, "Seeing the Bible Come Alive!"

Seeing the Bible Come Alive!

1. Read the words of encouragement that John speaks to the seven churches concerning the end of history when he speaks of the Lamb who is worthy to open the scroll found in *Revelation 5:1-14.*

2. Do Bible interpretation on this letter by analyzing this passage according to the Reading Strategies of Steps 1-4 and the Relating Strategies of Steps 5-7, as found below.

3. Remember to pray through each Step!

Reading Strategies:
Step 1: What kind of literary form is this Bible passage and what are the implications of this?

Step 2: What are the contextual boundaries of the Bible passage?

Step 3: What was God saying through this Bible passage to the original audience?

Step 4: What is the general principle that God had in mind through this Bible passage for all peoples and all cultures?

Relating Strategies:
Step 5: What is God saying through this Bible passage to you today?

Step 6: What is God saying through this Bible passage to your community of believers today?

Step 7: How will you communicate the truths of this Bible passage to your community of believers?

Appendix 2: Additional Discovery Bible Study Lessons

Discovering Leadership

Leaders Call Others to Follow Christ: *Matthew 4:18-25*
Leaders Teach Attitudes God Blesses: *Matthew 5:1-16; 6:33-34*
Leaders Seek to Please God: *Matthew 6:1-8, 16-18*
Leaders Serve God: Matthew 6:19-34
Leaders Judge Righteously: *Matthew 7:1-6; 18:15-20*
Leaders Seek God: *Matthew 7:7-12*
Leaders Obey God: *Matthew 7:21-29*
Leaders Care for Outcasts and Sinners: *Matthew 9:9-13*
Leaders Teach, Preach, and Heal: *Matthew 9:35-38*
Leaders Send People Out: *Matthew 10:1-16*
Leaders Prepare for Persecution: *Matthew 10:16-31*
Leaders Offer Rest to the Weary: *Matthew 11:25-30*
Leaders Teach About the Kingdom: *Matthew 13:1-9, 18-23*
Leaders Accept the Cost: *Matthew 16:13-28*
Leaders Listen to Jesus: *Matthew 17:1-13*
Leaders Teach About Faith: *Matthew 18:15-35*
Leaders Deal with Sin: *Matthew 18:15-35*
Leaders Honor Marriage: *Matthew 19:3-9*
Leaders are Servants: *Matthew 20:20-28*

Discovering Church Planting

Love and Obedience: *Matthew 22:24-40*
Love and Obedience: *Deuteronomy 6:1-6*
Love and Obedience: *John 14:15-26*
The Great Commission: *Matthew 28:16-20*
Draw People to Christ: *John 12:20-33*
Draw People to Christ: *John 20:21*
Draw People to Christ: *Philippians 2:1-11*
Draw People to Christ: *1 Corinthians 9:1-27*
Overcoming Barriers - Part 1: *Acts 10:9-48*
Overcoming Barriers - Part 1: *Acts 1:8*
Overcoming Barriers - Part 2: *Matthew 28:18-20*
Overcoming Barriers - Part 2: *Acts 17:15-34*

Overcoming Barriers - Part 3: *Mark 16:15-16*
Overcoming Barriers - Part 3: *Acts 28:1-10*
Overcoming Barriers - Part 4: *Luke 24:45-49*
Overcoming Barriers - Part 4: *Luke 24:13-27*
Overcoming Barriers - Part 5: *John 20:21*
Overcoming Barriers - Part 5: *Acts 13:1-4*
Overcoming Barriers - Part 6: *John 18:15-27*
Overcoming Barriers - Part 6: *John 21:15-19*
Spiritual Warfare - Part 1: *Ephesians 6:10-18*
Spiritual Warfare - Part 2: *2 Chronicles 20:1-30*
Spiritual Warfare - Part 3: *Exodus 17:8-16*
Spiritual Warfare - Part 4: *Matthew 24:9-14*
Imitate Christ: *1 Corinthians 4:1-17*
Imitate Christ: *1 Corinthians 10:3-11:1*
Person of Peace: *Luke 9:1-6*
Person of Peace: *Luke 10:1-20*
Appropriate Evangelism: *Matthew 10:5-20*
Appropriate Evangelism: *Acts 16:11-15*
Spiritual Community: *Matthew 28:19-20*
Spiritual Community: *1 Corinthians 12:12-20*
Spiritual Community: *Matthew 16:13-21*
Spiritual Community: *Acts 2:41-47*
Leadership – Part 1: *Ezekiel 34*
Leadership – Part 2: *1 Peter 5:1-11*
Leadership – Part 3: *Matthew 23:1-39*
Functions of Church: *1 Chronicles 16:7-36*

Discovering Obedience

Luke 4:1-13

Luke 5:1-11

John 4:28-30

Acts 17:16-34

Acts 4:23-31

Acts 21:1-14

Acts 18:1-11

Luke 15: 11-32

Mark 7:14-23

Matthew 19:1-12

Acts 5:1-11

I Samuel 24

Matthew 5:43-48

Luke 18:9-14

Luke 15:11-24

Matthew 26:39-42

Appendix 3: Bible Reading Plan

The following pages include Bible Reading Guides:

Old Testament Reading Guide:

Every day, listen or read one chapter from the Old Testament. You will complete the full Old Testament in three years because it has 929 chapters. Each chapter you read, cross the number for that chapter.

New Testament Reading Guide:

Every day, listen or read one chapter from the New Testament. You will complete the full New Testament in only 260 days because it has only 260 chapters. Each chapter you read, cross the number for that chapter.

Old Testament	
Genesis	1 2 3 4 5 6 7 8 9 10 11 12 13 14 15 16 17 18 19 20 21 22 23 24 25 26 27 28 29 30 31 32 33 34 35 36 37 38 39 40 41 42 43 44 45 46 47 48 49 50
Exodus	1 2 3 4 5 6 7 8 9 10 11 12 13 14 15 16 17 18 19 20 21 22 23 24 25 26 27 28 29 30 31 32 33 34 35 36 37 38 39 40
Leviticus	1 2 3 4 5 6 7 8 9 10 11 12 13 14 15 16 17 18 19 20 21 22 23 24 25 26 27
Numbers	1 2 3 4 5 6 7 8 9 10 11 12 13 14 15 16 17 18 19 20 21 22 23 24 25 26 27 28 29 30 31 32 33 34 35 36
Deuteronomy	1 2 3 4 5 6 7 8 9 10 11 12 13 14 15 16 17 18 19 20 21 22 23 24 25 26 27 28 29 30 31 32 33 34
Joshua	1 2 3 4 5 6 7 8 9 10 11 12 13 14 15 16 17 18 19 20 21 22 23 24
Judges	1 2 3 4 5 6 7 8 9 10 11 12 13 14 15 16 17 18 19 20 21
Ruth	1 2 3 4
1 Samuel	1 2 3 4 5 6 7 8 9 10 11 12 13 14 15 16 17 18 19 20 21 22 23 24 25 26 27 28 29 30 31
2 Samuel	1 2 3 4 5 6 7 8 9 10 11 12 13 14 15 16 17 18 19 20 21 22 23 24
1 Kings	1 2 3 4 5 6 7 8 9 10 11 12 13 14 15 16 17 18 19 20 21 22
2 Kings	1 2 3 4 5 6 7 8 9 10 11 12 13 14 15 16 17 18 19 20 21 22 23 24 25
1 Chronicles	1 2 3 4 5 6 7 8 9 10 11 12 13 14 15 16 17 18 19 20 21 22 23 24 25 26 27 28 29
2 Chronicles	1 2 3 4 5 6 7 8 9 10 11 12 13 14 15 16 17 18 19 20 21 22 23 24 25 26 27 28 29 30 31 32 33 34 35 36
Ezra	1 2 3 4 5 6 7 8 9 10

Nehemiah	1 2 3 4 5 6 7 8 9 10 11 12 13
Esther	1 2 3 4 5 6 7 8 9 10
Job	1 2 3 4 5 6 7 8 9 10 11 12 13 14 15 16 17 18 19 20 21 22 23 24 25 26 27 28 29 30 31 32 33 34 35 36 37 38 39 40 41 42
Psalms	1 2 3 4 5 6 7 8 9 10 11 12 13 14 15 16 17 18 19 20 21 22 23 24 25 26 27 28 29 30 31 32 33 34 35 36 37 38 39 40 41 42 43 44 45 46 47 48 49 50 51 52 53 54 55 56 57 58 59 60 61 62 63 64 65 66 67 68 69 70 71 72 73 74 75 76 77 78 79 80 81 82 83 84 85 86 87 88 89 90 91 92 93 94 95 96 97 98 99 100 101 102 103 104 105 106 107 108 109 110 111 112 113 114 115 116 117 118 119 120 121 122 123 124 125 126 127 128 129 130 131 132 133 134 135 136 137 138 139 140 141 142 143 144 145 146 147 148 149 150
Proverbs	1 2 3 4 5 6 7 8 9 10 11 12 13 14 15 16 17 18 19 20 21 22 23 24 25 26 27 28 29 30 31
Ecclesiastes	1 2 3 4 5 6 7 8 9 10 11 12
Song of Songs	1 2 3 4 5 6 7 8
Isaiah	1 2 3 4 5 6 7 8 9 10 11 12 13 14 15 16 17 18 19 20 21 22 23 24 25 26 27 28 29 30 31 32 33 34 35 36 37 38 39 40 41 42 43 44 45 46 47 48 49 50 51 52 53 54 55 56 57 58 59 60 61 62 63 64 65 66
Jeremiah	1 2 3 4 5 6 7 8 9 10 11 12 13 14 15 16 17 18 19 20 21 22 23 24 25 26 27 28 29 30 31 32 33 34 35 36 37 38 39 40 41 42 43 44 45 46 47 48 49 50 51 52
Lamentations	1 2 3 4 5
Ezekiel	1 2 3 4 5 6 7 8 9 10 11 12 13 14 15 16 17 18 19 20 21 22 23 24 25 26 27 28 29 30 31 32 33 34 35 36 37 38 39 40 41 42 43 44 45 46 47 48

Daniel	1 2 3 4 5 6 7 8 9 10 11 12
Hosea	1 2 3 4 5 6 7 8 9 10 11 12 13 14
Joel	1 2 3
Amos	1 2 3 4 5 6 7 8 9
Obadiah	1
Jonah	1 2 3 4
Micah	1 2 3 4 5 6 7
Nahum	1 2 3
Habakkuk	1 2 3
Zephaniah	1 2 3
Haggai	1 2
Zechariah	1 2 3 4 5 6 7 8 9 10 11 12 13 14
Malachi	1 2 3 4

New Testament	
Matthew	1 2 3 4 5 6 7 8 9 10 11 12 13 14 15 16 17 18 19 20 21 22 23 24 25 26 27 28
Mark	1 2 3 4 5 6 7 8 9 10 11 12 13 14 15 16
Luke	1 2 3 4 5 6 7 8 9 10 11 12 13 14 15 16 17 18 19 20 21 22 23 24
John	1 2 3 4 5 6 7 8 9 10 11 12 13 14 15 16 17 18 19 20 21
Acts	1 2 3 4 5 6 7 8 9 10 11 12 13 14 15 16 17 18 19 20 21 22 23 24 25 26 27 28
Romans	1 2 3 4 5 6 7 8 9 10 11 12 13 14 15 16
1 Corinthians	1 2 3 4 5 6 7 8 9 10 11 12 13 14 15 16
2 Corinthians	1 2 3 4 5 6 7 8 9 10 11 12 13
Galatians	1 2 3 4 5 6
Ephesians	1 2 3 4 5 6
Philippians	1 2 3 4
Colossians	1 2 3 4
1 Thessalonians	1 2 3 4 5
2 Thessalonians	1 2 3
1 Timothy	1 2 3 4 5 6
2 Timothy	1 2 3 4
Titus	1 2 3
Philemon	1
Hebrews	1 2 3 4 5 6 7 8 9 10 11 12 13
James	1 2 3 4 5
1 Peter	1 2 3 4 5
2 Peter	1 2 3
1 John	1 2 3 4 5
2 John	1
3 John	1
Jude	1
Revelation	1 2 3 4 5 6 7 8 9 10 11 12 13 14 15 16 17 18 19 20 21 22

Made in the USA
Middletown, DE
25 February 2023